MORE THAN 101 GREAT IDEAS

Strategies for spiritual and moral development in the RE classroom

Rosemary Rivett

Contents

Purchasing institutions may download the online resources PDF by visiting the RE Today Services website at www.retoday.org.uk/101greatideas and entering the password 101SSMDRE.

Introduction

Ten important questions about active learning and the brain

1 Why bother with active learning?

There are many reasons why teaching should be active in the classroom:

- It will be more interesting for pupils and teachers.
- It can help pupils to process the ideas rather than simply regurgitate them.
- It will open up the possibility of new thinking and creativity, getting pupils to stretch their thinking beyond their own experience.
- It can suit the needs of a range of different personalities, characters, abilities and ages in the classroom.

There is no substitute for thoughtful planning and the use of rich and stimulating content, of course, but active learning can contribute to good learning.

There is some evidence to suggest that the major impact of many classroom interventions is down to teacher enthusiasm, rather than the benefits of the intervention itself. Your energy and enthusiasm in the classroom are vital, and developing active learning with your pupils can both reveal and support this.

2 What does learning do to the brain?

Neuroscience reveals that our brains are flexible and adaptable – your pupils' brains even more so. Brain plasticity means that our brains are physically altered by experiences as connections are made between neurones. These connections grow stronger if the experience is repeated, so that practice enables the connections to strengthen.

This process has been compared to a path through the woods: at first a new action or piece of knowledge is difficult to learn, as if you have to push your way through the undergrowth. Gradually, as you repeat the action or go over the knowledge, it becomes easier, until eventually the connection is so strong that you can perform the action or recall the information without effort. Think about how you learned to drive – what a complicated process it seemed to be! And yet now there are probably times when you arrive at your destination without being able to recall making all those crucial decisions. The brain connections are fast and established.

Think about the implications for your pupils: they (and you) should expect a struggle at the start of a new skill or topic, but perseverance and practice will pay off.

Make some new connections and read this excellent report from the Teaching and Learning Research Programme: www.tlrp.org/pub/documents/Neuroscience%20Commentary%20FINAL.pdf

3 What difference does it make, knowing your brain is flexible?

The impact on pupils of knowing that their brains grow and strengthen is notable. Carole Dweck argues that many pupils have a fixed mindset – they believe that they have a certain amount of intelligence, and that's that. This means that challenges become threatening for these pupils as they believe that they might not be able to cope, and mistakes and failure become demoralising because they believe that such failures show that they do not have sufficient intelligence.

Other students have an incremental view of intelligence – 'growth mindsets'. It follows the brain science that our brains are flexible, that they grow and develop connections. These pupils see that effort and education help develop this potential intelligence and ability. For these pupils, facing challenges, making mistakes and keeping going in the face of setbacks are all ways of increasing their intelligence – of making more, better, faster connections in their brain – connections that last. Carol Dweck's research shows that if pupils understand that they can grow their intelligence, they can make significant improvements in learning.

Learn about the research by reading Dweck's short article 'Brainology':

www.nais.org/Magazines-Newsletters/ISMagazine/Pages/Brainology.aspx

4 How can we help pupils pay attention?

You probably know from your own experience that you have at least two types of attention. Sometimes you are at the mercy of any distraction, and any sudden noise makes you turn your head. This is a kind of instinctive attention that is stimulated by novelty or intensity. This is vital to enable us to react quickly to danger, for example. At other times you seem able to focus on a task at hand, time passes without you noticing, background noises fade away.

This ability to control and direct our attention is often referred to by neuroscientists as 'executive function'. It is usually linked with the frontal cortex of the brain, which exercises a co-ordinating role with other sections of the brain. Executive function plays a part in decision-making, planning, shifting our attention, inhibiting interference from external as well as internal distractions, and handles our working memory – those handful of ideas that we hold at the front of our mind when we are concentrating on an activity.

With young children, the instinctive attention dominates. Gradually, as children develop, they have to learn to exercise their executive function and direct their attention. You will know from your classroom experience that it is not a straightforward process: children can easily be distracted. However, supporting children in the development of this complex ability to direct and control their attention, and resist interference, is vital.

With a title like 'executive function' it might appear as if we are able to maintain control of our attention, but Jonathan Haidt points out that it is a little like a rider on an elephant – it has some measure of control, but at any moment our instinctive or emotional brain can go its own way!

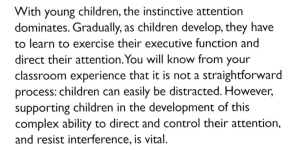

You might like to explore the famous 'marshmallow experiment', which reveals the long-term impact of developing executive function and controlling desires: www.ted.com/talks/joachim_de_posada_says_don_t_eat_the_marshmallow_yet.html

5 What are some good ways to enable good learning?

Consider how you need to think (a) when facing a question in a test, and (b) when facing a personal ethical dilemma.

According to neuroscientist Elkhonen Goldberg, there is a difference between the kinds of brain processes needed for (a) or *veridical decision-making*, where the goal is to find the correct answer to a problem, and the processes needed for (b) or *adaptive decision-making*. This is when we have to co-ordinate our personal responses to new situations, and where there may be no single correct response. The first requires recall and identification of a correct response; the second requires a sophisticated use of executive function, co-ordinating memory, prediction, imagination and creative application of ideas, along with our beliefs.

The findings of neuroscience suggest that adaptive decision-making is both more demanding and also more valuable in terms of learning. It requires pupils to make appropriate choices in ambiguous situations. Setting your pupils open-ended enquiries, real-life situations and problem-based activities, and allowing them to explore and apply what they have learned, will develop learning more effectively than rote memorisation.

Here's a review of Elkhonen Goldberg's book, *The New Executive Brain* (New York 2009), ISBN 9780195329407, which explains the key ideas: www.americanscientist.org/bookshelf/pub/decisions-decisions

6 Is learning a conscious activity?

A controversial experiment in the 1990s revealed the hidden impact of words. Experimenters set people a series of tasks to rearrange a series of words into simple sentences. Researchers found that if the sentences included words to do with being old, the subjects walked more slowly to the door when they had finished the task than if the words included reference to youth, vigour and energy.

John Bargh claims that words can 'prime' our behaviour, and this is reinforced by findings in neuroscience that most mental processes happen automatically, without conscious attention and control. The so-called 'nudge' theory backs this up – it is easier to change people's behaviour by nudging them to make choices rather than directing them. If this is correct, it shows how important it is that we set up a good ethos in our classrooms with our use of display, our own use of language and actions, and the kinds of texts we use within our lessons.

You can find John Bargh's original 1996 paper through his website: http://bargh.socialpsychology.org/publications and information about 'Nudge' on this 20-minute video: www.thersa.org/events/video/archive/richard-thaler

7 Must active learning be noisy?

You probably have some splendid extrovert pupils in your classes. They make a great contribution to lessons with their energy and their willingness to contribute. You've certainly noticed that some pupils are quieter, and you try to draw them out and involve them in active learning. But we should do more to encourage the quietness of these quiet pupils.

There is evidence of the value of introversion in the classroom. Recent research shows the value of allowing pupils to have freedom to work alone. It is not that introverts are shy, but they seek different kinds of stimulation – internal rather than external. Group work can often be dominated by extroverts; brainstorming has been shown to be less effective in producing creative responses than individuals thinking for themselves; so we should balance group work with quiet reflection and contemplation, and individual learning. As Susan Cain puts it, we should 'go into the wilderness' a little more.

Susan Cain's book, *Quiet: Introverts in a World that Can't Stop Talking* (London 2013), ISBN 9780141029191, explores this area. Listen to her give a short summary of her ideas here: www.ted.com/talks/susan_cain_the_power_of_introverts.html

8 Can I believe everything I hear about neuroscience and learning?

It is important to know that some ideas from neuroscience have been introduced to the classroom with very little evidence to back them up. For example:

(a) Left-brain–right-brain: This is the idea that left brain is logical/linear and right brain is creative/intuitive. However, our brains are so much more complicated than this – both hemispheres are in action all the time.

(b) Neurokinaesthetics: The idea that doing specific exercises stimulates specific parts of the brain has no evidence to back it up. So claims about certain 'gym' exercises for the brain are without foundation. However, general exercise does stimulate blood flow around the brain, and this can be good for keeping us awake!

(c) Visual/auditory/kinaesthetic learning styles: The idea that we all have preferred styles of learning is not backed up by neuroscience. Some argue that this applies to Gardner's Theory of Multiple Intelligences, too. However, as pupils have different abilities, using a variety of ways of communicating concepts, embedding ideas and practising skills may well help your pupils.

There is a danger of making unsubstantiated recommendations on the basis of limited neuroscientific evidence. This book is not intended to do this, but to encourage teachers to explore different ways of teaching to meet the needs of the pupils in their own classes.

John Geake writes thoughtfully about cognitive neuroscience. His brief outline, 'Neuromythologies in Education', is available online. His book, *The Brain at School: Educational Neuroscience in the Classroom* (London 2009), ISBN 9780335234219, is an extended exploration of neuroscience and education.

9 Are there good ways of building connections in the brain?

All activities affect our neurones, and learning is a very complex process, so there are no simple summaries that capture it. However, if you think about the most memorable experiences in your own life, they may well be associated with several senses: moments of high emotion are linked with sounds and smells – think of how certain smells take you right back to an event like a celebration, or the start of a youthful romance; or how strong the memory is of when you were involved in or

close to an accident – sounds, sensations, smells, visuals – all can be vividly recalled. There was a recent news report of someone using a different deodorant for each holiday he went on, so that later on he could have a whiff of the deodorant and be transported back to the different holidays! So, in order to develop our ability to make connections, our lessons might explore using the range of senses, for example: the taste of honey and of bitter herbs used in the Pesach meal; using incense and music; doing meditative exercises; practising stillness. How about coloured paper for different parts of a topic, or listening to the same song for each section of revision?

10 What difference does this make to how we plan our RE curriculum?

This section of our book on active learning has been about some implications of neuroscience and psychology for teaching and learning. It is worth remembering that insights on curriculum design can also help teachers. Jerome Bruner proposed that any subject can be taught 'in some intellectually honest form to any child at any stage of development' (Bruner 1960, p.33) – that we should not assume that some subjects are too difficult. He suggested that a 'spiral curriculum' is put in place, where basic concepts are revisited repeatedly as children progress through the school. This will allow pupils to develop their learning, constructing a more sophisticated understanding. So, a conceptual approach to RE, exploring concepts from shared human experience and linking with specifically religious concepts, would fit with this 'spiral curriculum'.

This approach relates well to the understanding of how the brain works, by making connections. We should be ensuring that our classrooms are places where abundant neural connections are made, challenging pupils to encounter novel situations, practise skills, revisit ideas and information and express their understanding in a variety of ways. We should be encouraging active learning!

Jerome Bruner's brief book, *The Process of Education*, (Cambridge, Mass. 1960), ISBN 9780674710016, is still available and worth a read!

Ten important questions about spiritual and moral development

1 What is spirituality?

This is a difficult term to pin down to the satisfaction of everyone, but so are many other terms! For example, is there an accepted definition of human nature, or goodness, or truth? Different religious and non-religious worldviews offer varying accounts of spirituality and so it will always be contested. Within schools the description of the spiritual needs to be suited to plural learning communities.

To get started, here are some comments from four 11-year-old pupils in answer to the question 'What is spirituality?'

- It's there and it's not there. (Martin)
- It's about not being empty inside. (Maxine)
- It's not just about me. (Sara)
- It's about changing our world. (Peter)

These statements capture something of the elusive nature of spirituality as well as its part in a person's inner life. But these ideas are balanced by the comments that spirituality is also about relationships with others and about having an impact on the world. Spiritual development is about changing how people live, not just how they think and feel.

2 What might a spiritually developed person be like?

Clive Beck has drawn up a list of characteristics of spiritually developing people that are widely shared between different religions and philosophies. He suggests that people who are developing spiritually will value these qualities:

- love
- awareness
- a broad mind
- a holistic outlook
- integration (avoiding hypocrisy)
- wonder
- thankfulness
- hope
- courage
- energy
- detachment
- acceptance
- gentleness

Clearly this is neither definitive nor exhaustive, but it paints a picture of the kind of person that many people from diverse traditions would aspire to be like. It is a helpful starting-point when thinking about spiritual development in schools.

3 How is spirituality connected to religion?

Within each religion, there is spiritual diversity. Buddhists may be engaged in expressing their faith through social concern, or more interested in meditation practice, or seek to unite the two. Christians might exercise the 'gifts of the Spirit' in their daily lives and worship, or serve God by striving for justice, or see their spiritual life as one of contemplation – or all three. Each tradition has its conservatives and liberals, its fundamentalists and radicals. Each tradition contains many spiritualities. There are also many spiritualities that overflow from religion to wider communities, and some that come from non-religious sources.

4 Can you be spiritual and not religious?

Beyond religion, a high proportion of young people, particularly, sign up to the idea of being spiritual but not religious. This also means many things, but the gathering of commitment around spirituality for the non-religious should be taken very seriously by the RE teacher.

One useful way of looking at this complexity is the idea, put forward by David Hay and Rebecca Nye in *The Spirit of the Child*, that each person has their own spiritual signature, a way of looking at human identity that is as individual as a fingerprint. This insight might require teachers of RE to take the broadest possible view of spiritual identity. Certainly, it is wise to look for spirituality both within and beyond religions. Some Humanists are happy to describe a spiritual dimension to their lives, but other Humanists deny this, and suggest that you can describe human nature without any need for a category of 'spirituality'.

5 What is the place of spiritual and moral development in schools?

All state-funded schools and academies must offer a curriculum that is balanced and broadly based and that promotes the spiritual, moral, cultural, mental and physical development of pupils at the school and of society, and prepares pupils at the school for the opportunities, responsibilities and experiences of later life (Section 78, 2002 Education Act; Section 1, 2010 Academies Act). This legislation places pupils' spiritual and moral development at the heart of the purpose of education. Schooling and the curriculum should address spiritual and moral development through the whole ethos of the school as well as the curriculum, with RE playing a particular role.

Just as English leads on literacy, with all subjects contributing to its development, so RE can lead with regard to spirituality, with all subjects contributing to pupils' spiritual and moral development. Drama, English, History, PE, Art and Music can all provide pupils with wonderful opportunities for spiritual development, but in RE these are most often at the core of the learning. The RE teacher who can excite colleagues and learners about life's spiritual dimension can build an effective and significant place for the subject in the school's life as a whole.

6 What might school spiritual and moral development look like?

Here are two descriptions which might form the starting-point for teachers to reflect on their understanding within their own schools:

Spiritual development enables people to look within themselves, at their human relationships, at the wider world and, for many, at their vision of the divine or the ultimate reality with characteristics such as courage, hope, acceptance, strength and love, so that they can better face the sufferings, challenges and opportunities of human life in all its fullness.

Moral development enables pupils to take an increasingly thoughtful view of what is right and wrong, to recognise the needs and interests of others as well as themselves and develop characteristics such as truthfulness, kindness, unselfishness, and commitments to virtues such as integrity, justice and the will to do what is right, so that they can live in ways that respect the wellbeing and rights of each person.

7 What kinds of curriculum content and classroom activities might give opportunities for spiritual and moral development?

At the heart of spiritual development for pupils is the encounter with people, stories, art and actions that can challenge their understanding of the world and of themselves. In this sense, almost any content can contribute to spiritual development. What is required is for teachers to set up a context where the pupils interact with the content in such a way that it can have an impact on their thoughts, feelings, intuitions and actions. It presupposes that learning is not a passive activity whereby information is presented to be memorised. Spiritual development requires an active encounter, giving the possibility of pupils' response, although not insisting upon it. For example, considering how and why some religious believers have demonstrated the characteristics of spiritual development from question 2 in this section, and how and why some have not, can lead to pupils considering their own behaviour and motivations.

8 How do we know if pupils are doing well in these areas?

It is not possible or appropriate to assess spirituality and morality in the same way as assessing knowledge, skills and understanding. A more suitable and useful approach is for teachers to be clear about the opportunities they provide for developing spiritual insights and to monitor these thoughtfully but informally. Many teachers will find it worth using some self-assessment with pupils, asking them 'What was the most spiritual piece of work you did in RE this term?' Collecting a folio of work from pupils in answer to this question will gradually show and develop your RE department's practice in this crucial area. Where the subject curriculum addresses spiritual issues using the skills of empathy, reflection, conceptual analysis, creative imagination and developing insight, learners often respond enthusiastically to challenging ideas and activities. It marks out spiritual RE from being concerned only with examination success or high grades.

Evidence of pupil personal development can be revealed through actions. Involvement in school and community projects, charitable fundraising, voluntary work or serving others are all valuable outcomes of spiritual and moral development. An Ofsted document from 2004 (*Promoting and Evaluating Pupils' Spiritual, Moral, Social and Cultural Development*, Ofsted 2004) states that a spiritually developed person will be ready to stand against anything that constrains the human spirit, such as moral neutrality or indifference, aggression, greed, injustice, self-interest, sexism, racism and other forms of discrimination. Community involvement is one expression of this concern for the wellbeing of others.

9 Is spiritual and moral development good for pupils?

Debates may rage about education policy and the value of rote learning or pupil-centred curricula, but there is little argument that schools should aim to develop the whole child, not simply the cognitive faculties.

Consider the question: 'What characteristics would a spiritually and morally stunted pupil possess?' Schools clearly reject the idea that they would or should be content to contribute to that outcome. Schools show on-going concern with pupils' character, wellbeing, resilience, motivation, attitudes, and with their sense of meaning and purpose. This is the motivation for most teachers, to help develop pupils and prepare them for adult life through a rich experience of learning subjects, building relationships, taking responsibility, making moral choices, and much more. A focus on spiritual and moral development reflects the intentions of most schools and teachers and underpins these wider school aims.

This is not to say, of course, that schools can guarantee pupils' spiritual or moral development! As with most personal development in learning, progress is unlikely to be linear, often likely to be episodic, and quite possibly with many backward steps. As a result, the key is for schools to be offering a wide variety of opportunities for personal development and allowing for the varied progress of pupils. After all, which teacher can claim an untroubled journey in personal growth throughout their life?

10 How can RE support pupils' social development?

Social development includes enabling pupils to relate to others within a variety of communities. It involves developing social skills, qualities, attitudes and characteristics such as respect, acceptance of difference, and a willingness to be active in their communities.

RE makes a rich contribution through its exploration of diverse beliefs and practices, within and between religious and non-religious communities. It supports social development through the central place of pupils reflecting on their own ideas, attitudes and actions in response to their learning about religions and beliefs. The content of the RE curriculum deals with the value of diverse communities as responses to shared human experiences, as well as facing up to the real challenges of living in a world of difference.

11 How can RE support pupils' cultural development?

Promoting cultural development includes giving opportunities to develop pupils' awareness and understanding of their own identity and place in society, and to help them to value and participate creatively in their own culture and the culture of others. It also involves developing their appreciation of diverse aspects of culture, such as the arts, language and customs.

RE explores a diversity of cultural expressions as seen in religious traditions, revealing the richness of human expression, whether through art, music, poetry, literature, architecture, dance, theatre, ritual or activism. These diverse expressions can convey key concepts, beliefs and practices, and pupils can be encouraged to express their own understanding and reflections creatively.

Pupils can encounter some of the most profound responses to the human condition through sacred texts, religious art and music, rituals and actions. A growing understanding of cultural diversity can play a part in helping pupils to grasp their own identity and to respond with sensitivity and insight to others.

Enquiry in RE

One important part of active learning is encouraging and enabling pupils to become enquirers in RE – supporting them in asking deep questions and giving them the skills to begin to explore them. The value of enquiry has been expressed in many places, but notably in the Ofsted report, *Transforming Religious Education* (2010).

Promoting challenging learning is 'related primarily to engaging pupils with stimulating ideas and enquiries in ways that encouraged independent thought and reflection. Pupils were challenged in RE when, for example, they:

- linked aspects of their learning together
- designed and carried out their own investigations into beliefs and practices
- interpreted and challenged religious material such as stories, images or metaphors
- used skills such as prediction, speculation or evaluation
- engaged with some of the more evocative, personal and imaginative dimensions of religion and belief, relating these to their own lives
- used talk, writing and the arts to express their ideas and responses.'

Transforming Religious Education (Religious education in schools, 2006–2009), Ofsted 2010. This report built on the findings of an earlier report *Making Sense of Religion.*

There are many models of enquiry in education but the process on the following page takes the RE skills often identified in locally agreed syllabuses and clusters them, so that pupils have an opportunity to develop many skills during one enquiry. It is designed as a pupil process, and so uses terms that pupils can understand. It is also designed to suit pupils of different age groups, because it is clear that young pupils are able to begin a process of interpretation, albeit at a simple level. For example, the ability to suggest meanings of words or stories leads onto a more developed ability to draw out meanings from images, texts or actions, which leads on to the more sophisticated ability to interpret different sources and understand ways in which believers interpret sacred texts.

The use of 'personal' and 'impersonal' evaluation resurrects the ideas of Michael Grimmitt, from whose work the concepts of 'learning about' and 'learning from 'religion are derived. In his book, *RE and Human Development*, Grimmitt (1987) pointed out that good learning in RE involves an interaction between the pupil and the religious material, so that they learn about religion and learn from religion about themselves.

Learning *about* religion includes beliefs, teachings and practices of religious traditions, the nature of faith responses to ultimate questions, and the shaping influence of religious beliefs and values on cultural and personal histories.

Learning *from* religion is where pupils take their understanding of religion and apply it to what they learn about themselves, in order to clarify their values, for example, or to critically evaluate truth claims. This critical evaluation includes:

- impersonal evaluation, that is 'being able to distinguish and make critical evaluations of truth claims, beliefs and practices of different religious traditions and of religion itself' (Grimmitt 1987, p.225) and

- personal evaluation, which 'begins as an attempt to confront and evaluate religious beliefs and values [and] becomes a process of self-evaluation' (Grimmitt 1987, p.226).

The enquiry process on the following page incorporates this into the process of learning in RE.

Many of the strategies in the following pages of *More Than 101 Great Ideas* are appropriate for the 'investigate' stage of the enquiry process in particular.

Michael Grimmitt's book is still worth reading, for those who want a deep insight into the purposes and processes of RE: *RE and Human Development*, (Great Wakering 1987) ISBN 9780855974015

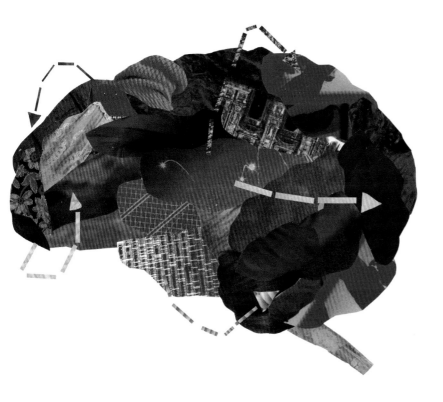

A model for enquiry in RE

Using clusters of RE skills, teachers can use this process in their own planning of lessons or units, or for structuring pupil-led enquiries.

Ask questions
Set up an enquiry

1 **Reflect** on stimulus material
2 **Ask** questions
3 **Analyse** questions, in relation to RE fields of enquiry
4 **Evaluate** questions, resulting in selecting focus question(s), with reasons for choice

This section might be done in the style of Philosophy for Children, with pupils devising the questions. Alternatively, this process could be part of the teacher's planning, and the enquiry process for pupils starts with **investigate.**

Investigate
Select from and use a variety of skills to work with relevant material to address the enquiry question

Select relevant materials
Select skills, depending upon nature of focus question(s)

suggest meanings	sort ideas	make links	reflect on impact on self
draw out meanings	explain similarities and differences	explain connections	reflect on impact on self and others
interpret sources	analyse ideas	come up with coherent synthesis	develop empathise to deepen understanding

At this point it is a good idea to establish some learning outcomes in the form of levelled 'I can' statements. Teachers can do this with pupils.

Not all skills will be used in every enquiry, but it will be necessary to set up certain interactions with the material to enable the skills to be practised. For example, **interpretation** requires some original source material, a chance to suggest meanings and a way of comparing it with some religious interpretations.

Evaluate
Weigh up arguments and assess conclusions

Impersonal (critical) **evaluation:**
Think about reasons, ponder possibilities, argue, come to tentative conclusions, weigh up and justify conclusion(s)

Personal **evaluation:**
Discern the value and significance of learning from religion: do or should these ideas and conclusions have an impact on my life? Handle tentative responses and ambiguity

Both elements are part of attainment target 2, learning from religion and belief. Both elements are essential for good learning in RE.

Express
Articulate findings and their implications

Express findings – presenting alternative views and conclusions
Apply findings to myself and others, including the impact of findings on how I make sense of the world and how I live

Setting up a purpose for learning at an early stage in the enquiry may help give focus to the way pupils express ideas.

ACT

When learning is active, it is remembered, enjoyed and understood better. As the learners become involved in the process of their own learning they move to draw conclusions from their own thinking and reflection. Good RE places a high priority on active learning because passivity is a barrier to learning.

In this section you will find a wide variety of strategies that provide pupils with opportunities to express their ideas, understandings and questions in RE in an active and expressive way, for example through drama, freeze-frame, body sculpture, story, role play, mime, trust games, puppets, persona dolls and hotseating.

Many strategies could easily fit into one or more sections of this book. That's why each strategy is cross-referenced to others in the book that provide opportunities to develop some of the same aims, skills or opportunities.

There are pupil activity sheets to accompany some of the strategies; these are found in the online resources PDF. Sources of stories, images and films are found on the inside back cover.

1 Alphabet on the floor

Useful for

Introducing pupils to active strategies; enabling pupils to share some simple facts or deeper ideas about themselves; encouraging whole-class involvement.

See also

Affirmation–13
Post-its®–54

Strategy

- In a large space, lay out some A4 cards on the floor, each one with a letter of the alphabet written on it, as large as possible (it's useful to put P and Q together on the same card, and XYZ).
- Ask the group to stand around, and call out some prompt questions. They must think for five seconds, then go and place a foot on the initial letter of their answer. Invite them to tell the others who share their letter what their answer to the prompt question was, and say a bit about their answer. Usually letters like B, M, R, S or T have most people on them. Keep it moving: 6–10 prompts is enough.
- Questions (for a focus on spirituality) might include: What makes you feel peaceful? What is your favourite word? Who do you admire most from history? What's your most moving piece of music? How do you feel about God (one word)? What one thing do you do to save the earth?

2 Trust games

Useful for

Developing trust and collaboration within a group.

See also

Alphabet on the floor–1
Who am I?–12

Strategy

- Provide a safe learning environment, e.g. by supplying soft mats for landing.
- Choose one of the following:
    - Back to back: In pairs, A and B stand back to back and link through each other's arms. They then have to sit down and stand up together.
    - Blindfold find: All members of the group are blindfolded and put in different parts of the room. They have to link up with each other as quickly as possible. This is made more difficult if a 'no talking' rule is imposed.
    - Sitting circle: In groups of 10 or more, pupils form a circle, all facing clockwise, and then sit down in the lap of the person behind. If it is done correctly, everyone is supported by everyone else.

3 Trading places

Useful for

Engaging young children in learning in RE by using rich, evocative images of contemporary religious belief and practice and encouraging them to talk about what they see.

See also

Freeze-frame–5
Mystery bag–83
Through the keyhole–88

Strategy

- Show pupils an image or picture, e.g. a Christian baptism, Muslim men at prayer in a mosque, a Jewish family celebrating Hanukkah.
- Arrange pupils in groups and ask them to reproduce the image or picture, taking the place of people or characters in the photograph or artwork. As they put themselves in the position of the characters, facing the same way, using the same expressions, and so on, ask them what it feels like, and what might be going on in their character's mind and body.
- When they have brought the 2D image into 3D life, ask them to fast-forward five minutes – what position would people be in now? What reasons can they give?

4 Body sculpture

Strategy

- Arrange pupils in pairs with one taking the role of the sculptor and the other the 'clay'.
- Introduce the stimulus material and ask pupils to focus on the feelings or attitudes being expressed.
- The sculptors then 'mould' their partners to express the emotions or feelings they have identified in the stimulus material. Other pupils guess what inner feelings or attitudes are being expressed.
- Photograph the outcomes – these could provide a useful starting point for discussion with other groups or make an interesting wall display.

Useful for

Focusing pupils' thinking on the outward expression of inner feelings or attitudes, e.g. love, anger, hatred, forgiveness, injustice, as expressed by a narrative, text, poem, picture or video clip.

See also

Freeze-frame–5
Guided story–63
Feelings graph–97

5 Freeze-frame

Strategy

- Arrange pupils in small groups and read to them – or ask them to read for themselves – a story from a religious or belief tradition. For suggestions see p.79.
- Ask pupils to identify a key moment or turning point in the story. They should identify which characters are involved, allocate roles, and discuss what each might be thinking and feeling at the key moment. Together pupils work out and 'act out' a freeze-frame or 'still' image to depict the scene.
- Either 'catch the eye' or touch the shoulder of an individual who then shares the thoughts and feelings of their character 'in role'. Pupils can also ask questions of the character 'in role'.
- Use a digital camera to record the freeze-frames. This enables pupils to reflect on and record the thoughts and feelings of the characters in speech bubbles added to the image.

Useful for

Enabling pupils to 'get inside the story' to explore the feelings and experiences of key characters; developing skills of analysis, empathy and expression; developing group work and speaking and listening skills.

See also

Hotseat–17
Reflection alley–53
Box story–73
What really matters?–50

6 News bulletins

Strategy

- Arrange pupils in small groups and ask each group to prepare a one-minute radio or TV news bulletin on the lesson topic. Each group should elect a 'newsreader' who will read out the planned bulletin.
- Ask the 'newsreaders' to read out their group's bulletin. Each newsreader has just 60 seconds, and the bulletins should follow in quick succession.

Useful for

Consolidating pupils' learning from a lesson or series of lessons.

See also

Post-it®s–54
Yo-yo–75
Just a minute–85

7 RE-enactment

Strategy

- Arrange pupils in small groups and either read to them – or ask them to read for themselves – a story from a religious or belief tradition (see suggestions below and p.79).
- Pupils re-enact the event exactly as told in the story, trying to access its dynamics, relationships and meanings. The clearer and more detailed the stimulus material the better will be the results of the re-enactment.
- Pupils try presenting the story in different ways, e.g. angrily, happily, impatiently. They talk about how changing the mood affects how they understand the story.
- Draw out the deeper meaning of the story by using carefully planned probing questions, e.g.
  - How did it feel when …?
  - What did you think would happen after …?
  - Why do you think s/he said … did …?
  - What would have happened if …?

Examples of faith stories

- Buddhism: Kisagotami and the Mustard Seed; Angulimala and the Buddha
- Christianity: The Nativity; Pentecost
- Hinduism: Durga and the Buffalo Demon; The Story of Prahlad
- Judaism: Elijah and the Cave; Moses and the Ten Commandments
- Sikhism: Bhai Kanhaiya (Ghanaya); Sajjan the Thief.

8 Transporting a character

Strategy

- Arrange pupils in groups and ask them to brainstorm their ideas about a given character who is transported to a different place or time, or who interacts with a different set of characters, e.g. 'What if Jesus came to my home town today?'
- Encourage pupils to respond to questions such as: What would he say and do? Who would he see and talk to? What would he say? What would he do? What might he look like?
- Ask pupils to suggest what one piece of advice the chosen character might offer to the people he visited, and explain why.
- Other characters might include: the Buddha (Buddhism); Martin Luther King (Christianity); Mahatma Gandhi (Hinduism); the Prophet Muhammad (Islam); Guru Nanak (Sikhism). Remind pupils that the Prophet Muhammad (pbuh) and the Caliphs (Islam) should not be drawn. You might also include living characters, e.g. Aung San Suu Kyi (Buddhism); Archbishop Desmond Tutu (Christianity); Rabbi Hugo Gryn (Judaism); Yusuf Islam (Islam).

9 Role play

Strategy

- Arrange pupils in groups and introduce to them the situation you want them to role play. Clarify that they understand the details of the characters and situation involved. Providing cards with a brief summary of the situation on one side and a role description on the other is an effective way of ensuring everyone understands the role-play situation. See below for suggestions of possible situations.

- Explain that you want pupils to imagine they are in the situation and to pretend they are one of the characters involved. They should behave as they think that person would behave in the situation. Give pupils time to talk in their groups about what they will do and to rehearse their ideas before performing it.

- In the middle of the presentation consider using Freeze-frame as an opportunity for 'thought tapping'. The teacher freezes the improvisation and activates an individual by 'catching their eye' or tapping them on the shoulder. This allows pupils to speak aloud their private thoughts and reactions 'in role'.

- Provide structured reflective and expressive activities to follow the role play to explore insights stimulated in the role play. Follow-up questions might include:

  - What was happening in the role play?
  - How did the pupils feel (in role)?
  - What did pupils feel about each other's actions?
  - What did they learn from the role play?
  - What questions do pupils now have as a focus for future learning?

Examples of role-play situations

Faith Story
Pupils get inside a faith story by role-playing the action. They identify a key moment or a turning point in the story, identify the characters, and discuss what each would be feeling and doing. A digital camera can record key moments, and speech and thought bubbles added to the image express the ideas, thoughts and feelings of the characters.

Interviews and interrogation
Pupils take the role of journalists, detectives, scientists, TV or radio reporters, documentary film crews, jurors or police, to interview or question key figures involved in a given situation.

Meetings of decision-making bodies
Pupils simulate a meeting of an organisation, e.g. parish council; public enquiry; protest meeting; school governing body; school council; action group.

Overheard conversation
Hiding, spying and eavesdropping roles can explore themes like truth and lies, gossip, secrets and so on. Groups of three can develop overheard conversation.

Witness
Taking the role of a participant in an enquiry or trial, each person explains what he or she saw, heard and knew. This can be useful for exploring religious experience, for example Guru Nanak's disappearance (Sikhism) or Paul's conversion (Christianity).

RE Today Services 2013

Useful for
Arousing interest and active participation; using non-verbal communication skills; helping pupils understand the position and feelings of others, analysing a story or an incident; developing self-confidence.

See also

Freeze-frame–5

Writing my own report–10

Interviewing–43

Useful for

Encouraging reflection on achievements in RE; identifying aspects for improvement; taking responsibility for their own progress; developing self-awareness as a learner.

See also

Role play–9

Personal statement–66

Diary of reflection–104

Online resources PDF

10 Writing my own report

Strategy

- Provide pupils with a framework within which there is a choice of statements, expressed in sections, to respond to, relating to the work they have done, the learning opportunities they have had and the on-going feedback they have had from their peers and the teacher.

- Ask pupils to role-play the teacher writing a report. Pupils review their work in a particular unit of work, or over a given period of time, and are asked to write their own report in about 10 sentences. They should choose starters from five or more sections of the template (see example below and in the online resources PDF).

Writing my own report

This sheet is to help you write about the work you have been doing in RE.

Write as much as you can, but do at least 10 sentences, choosing starters from five or more boxes.

Think and write carefully on your own.

• This RE topic has made me think about … • Since doing this work in RE I have … • My reasons are … • I believe … • I can't make my mind up about … • Other people think …	• In RE we have been learning about … • What we've done in RE is … • Our lessons in RE have been about … • In RE I've learned about … • The main things I did in RE were …	• I could have improved my RE work by … • To do better in RE I will … • If I started this work again I would … • The effort I put in was … • I am most pleased with … • My RE written work is …
• I liked it when … • The best bit of the work was … • What I enjoyed about it was … • I found it interesting when … • The good thing about this work was …	• Now I understand more about … • Before doing this work in RE I didn't realise that … • One thing that made me think was … • It's surprising that … • I'm curious to find out more about … • I'm still puzzled about … • I can't be sure that … • One fascinating thing is …	• The advice I would give to someone starting this work would be … • Overall, my work has been … • From this work, I have gained … • Generally, RE has been … • Finally, I would like to say …

 Photocopy permission

11 Mime

Strategy

- Arrange pupils in pairs or small groups and ask them to devise a mime to represent the outward expression of an inner feeling (e.g. anger, sympathy) or moral virtue (e.g. goodness, generosity, compassion). Younger pupils could mime the feelings of characters in faith stories. Feelings are expressed through movement of the body and expression on the face.

- Encourage pupils to exaggerate the movements slightly. For younger pupils, suggest that they follow your lead to start off with, but are free to improvise their own actions. Older pupils can reflect more on what they are doing.

- If miming a story, pupils could: identify a key moment in a story; mime the experience to others; see if they can guess the moment; discuss what was happening and suggest why it was significant, and whether it was a 'turning point' in some way.

Useful for

Focusing attention; encouraging empathy and reflection; raising awareness of the power of inner feelings.

See also

Freeze-frame–5
Stilling–60

12 Who am I?

Strategy

- Give each member of the group a piece of card and ask them to write or draw four things which symbolise themselves, e.g. a football, a pet, a swimsuit, a pizza. When everyone is ready, collect the cards, shuffle and redistribute them.

- Pupils take it in turns to 'interpret' the symbols and words to work out who the card is describing.

- A variation could be to ask pupils to draw or write four things that symbolise something or someone they have studied in RE, e.g. a holy book, prayer beads, baptismal candle, a festival or celebration.

Useful for

Enabling pupils to share some simple facts or deeper ideas about themselves; encouraging empathy.

See also

Alphabet on the floor–1
Observation–58

13 Affirmation

Strategy

- Divide the class into three groups and number pupils in each group 1–10 (depending on the number in the group). Give each pupil a piece of paper and ask each to write his/her name on the top line.

- Pupils pass the papers to the next person in their group (i.e. 1 passes to 2, 2 passes to 3, and so on), who then writes a positive word or comment about person 1 on the bottom line. Person 2 folds the sheet up to hide the comment and passes it on to the next person. This continues around the room until the papers get back to the original owners.

- This activity makes a good starter activity in RE when:
  - introducing religious teaching on the special value of individuals, e.g. Adam (Judaism); being created in the image of God (Christianity)
  - learning about infant baptism (Christianity) or the aqiqah ceremony (Islam)
  - exploring the importance of names, e.g. the 99 beautiful names of God (Islam); the names of Jesus (Christianity).

Useful for

Developing self-esteem; encouraging honesty and sensitivity to others' feelings; introducing the idea of specialness, uniqueness or holiness.

See also

Feelings graph–97
Diary of reflection–104

Useful for

Helping younger pupils when retelling faith stories; engaging interest; as a distancing tool for pupils to express feelings; enabling the teacher to observe and analyse pupils' learning.

See also

Persona dolls–15

Box story–73

14 Puppets

Strategy

- Tell pupils a faith story, e.g. Jesus and Zacchaeus (Christianity); Sunita the Scavenger (Buddhism).
- Put pupils in small groups and tell them that they are going to create puppets to help them retell the story they have just heard for another audience. Give each group a section of the story to focus on.
- Provide pupils with the materials to create their puppets – one for each of the main characters in their section of the story. Suggestions for different types of puppets are given below. They should make sure that the puppets show the characteristics of the person in the story, e.g. Zacchaeus could look mean.
- Pupils practise acting out the story, ensuring that the main message of the story is included.
- Alternatively pupils can be given pre-cut silhouettes to present the story in front of the whiteboard.

Some simple ways of making your own puppets

- *Stick puppets:* Draw a face on stiff card, cut out and attach to a wooden stick or ruler. These can be silhouette, and used for shadow puppetry.
- *Paper bag puppets:* Use a bag 30cm x 15cm. Pupils draw faces, hair and clothes in strong bright colours. A 'head' could be made by stuffing the corner with crumpled paper and securing with an elastic band.
- *Glove puppets:* Cut out a simple shape from some strong fabric, to fit the hand of a child. Machine around the edge and turn inside out. Make a face with fabric pens or other materials.
- *Finger puppets:* Draw a face on a piece of paper. Make into a cylinder shape and secure with sticky tape. Some pupils could have two of these.

Useful for

Engaging young children with views, beliefs and ideas that may be different from their own; encouraging young children to ask questions and think through perspectives that may be new to them.

See also

Puppets–14

Bubbling speech...bubbling thoughts–52

Online resources PDF

15 Persona dolls

Strategy

- Start with a 3–4 minute introduction of the chosen persona doll by asking some questions and revisiting some earlier learning. For this example we have chosen Yusuf, a Muslim; the background information and prompt questions about him already shared with pupils are given in the online resources PDF. Questions for pupils might be:
  - Do you remember who this is?
  - Can you describe what Yusuf believes about Allah?
  - This week Yusuf is going to share with you how he prays (show a prayer mat, a picture or a real one). Before he prays he has a good wash. Why do you think Yusuf does this?
  - Are there times when you have a good wash?
  - What do you think Yusuf is thinking while he is praying?
  - What do you think he feels when he prays?
  - Are there any questions you would like to ask Yusuf?
- Allow as many pupils as possible an opportunity to respond – and finish on a positive note, e.g. 'You have learned so much about Yusuf and why he prays – well done!'
- To find out more see Shahne Vickery *Persona Dolls in Religious Education*, ISBN 9780955661129, available from http://shop.retoday.org.uk

16 Human barchart

Strategy

- Devise an opinions statement sheet made up of at least six controversial statements on the issue in question (see examples below and in the online resources PDF) and provide a copy for each pupil. Include numbers 1–6 underneath each statement (1 = strongly agree and 6 = strongly disagree) so that pupils can circle a number.

- Before the lesson begins, write the numbers 1–6 on A4 sheets and place them in a straight line on the floor or the wall of the classroom or corridor.

- Give pupils the opinions statement sheet and ask them to complete it privately, and anonymously, and in pencil. Pupils circle the number which most closely reflects their opinion for each statement. Encourage pupils to express their honest opinions by reassuring them that their responses will be completely anonymous.

- Each sheet is then folded in half, and half again, and exchanged five times.

- As the teacher reads out the statements, pupils line up in front of the number represented on the sheet they have been given, creating a human barchart.

- Pupils, working in groups, e.g. all those with 1 circled on their sheets, work out arguments to support the point of view they are representing. A good debate can arise between those who are 'strongly agreeing' and those who are 'strongly disagreeing'. Can they persuade others in the class to join them or will there be some defectors to the other side?

Useful for

Developing discussion and evaluation skills; encouraging expression of personal viewpoints while respecting privacy; enabling pupils to see arguments from other people's perspectives.

See also

Reflection alley–53
Snowballing–77
Snowflake–80
Online resources PDF

Wise Words	**Evil and Suffering**

Wise Words

Circle the number which best shows your response to each statement:

Strongly agree					**Strongly disagree**

Never try to get back at someone who makes you cry.

1	2	3	4	5	6

Worrying about what might happen is a waste of time.

1	2	3	4	5	6

Treat other people as you would like them to treat you.

1	2	3	4	5	6

Don't be greedy. Having lots of things won't make you safe and happy.

1	2	3	4	5	6

Evil and Suffering

Circle the number which best shows your response to each statement:

Strongly agree					**Strongly disagree**

Suffering is God's way of testing people.

1	2	3	4	5	6

God punishes the wicked and rewards the good.

1	2	3	4	5	6

Suffering is part of God's plan: we are unable to understand this.

1	2	3	4	5	6

Suffering has nothing to do with God.

1	2	3	4	5	6

Photocopy permission

Useful for

Consolidating learning; developing questioning and speaking & listening skills; a diagnostic activity for use in assessment.

See also

Visitors–46 & 47

Reflection alley–53

Balloon debate–79

Debate–81

17 Hotseat

Strategy

- Sit one member of the group centrally so that s/he can be seen by all members of the group, and can answer questions by the group. Give pupils time to think carefully about the questions they want to ask – and the person in the hotseat time to prepare.
- Pupils in the hotseat take on the role of a character they have studied and answer from the perspective of that person (not for themselves). Characters might include: Martin Luther King; Aung San Suu Kyi; Mahatma Gandhi; a disciple of Jesus; the Pope; Yusuf Islam; the Buddha; Moses.
  - With younger pupils this can conclude a unit of work, pupils working together to think up questions to ask and answers to give if they are in the hotseat.
  - With older pupils this activity should follow careful preparation – pupils may submit questions to the person in the hotseat (and his or her group of advisers) in advance so that they may do some research. Pupils' questions must arise from their own research.
- Visitors in the hotseat provide pupils with the opportunity to prepare their questions in advance. Brief the visitor carefully about how the visit fits in with the topic pupils are studying.
- When it's the teacher in the hotseat, ask pupils to research and prepare questions. They may work individually or in teams. When asking factual questions pupils must know the answer to the question. Teams may compete to see which is able to 'beat the teacher'!

Useful for

Getting the whole class involved and thinking; engaging reflection on personal responses to a situation or issue as a starting point for further exploration.

See also

Alphabet on the floor–1

Values auction–96

18 Everybody up!

Strategy

- Ask the class to stand up. Tell pupils to 'stay standing if …' At this point, have ready a series of statements connected to a particular topic. Everyone who has done this, thought this, wondered this, at any time stays standing; everyone else sits down. When a few are left standing, the teacher or a pupil interviews one or two people about their experiences.

Example: Exploring the issue of wealth and poverty

- Stay standing if you have ever:
  - asked your parents or carers for extra money
  - felt as though you were really missing out because you hadn't got the latest …
  - thought beggars should be cleared off the streets
  - felt a bit guilty eating your tea watching starving people on the news
  - put some money in a charity box
  - known someone who has tried to do something about the poor.

Example: Introducing some key teachings from religions and beliefs

- Stay standing if you have ever:
  - killed or hurt an animal and felt bad about it (e.g. Hinduism teaches that all life is one – it is the same divine spark in humans and animals)
  - seen someone 'lose it' in a big way in public, e.g. road rage or swearing (e.g. Buddhism teaches 'Conquer anger through gentleness. Be truthful and do not yield to anger.')
  - noticed a character in a 'Soap' who destroyed his/her own life (e.g. in Islam, Prophet Muhammad said 'There is a polish for everything that becomes rusty, and the polish for the human heart is remembering Allah.' *Hadith Tirmidhi*).

CREATE

Creative RE energises pupils' thinking, gives them time and opportunity to develop and express ideas and easily enables teamwork to flourish. Good RE needs more creative learning.

In this section you will find a wide variety of strategies that provide pupils with opportunities to express their ideas, understandings and questions in RE in a creative way, for example through art, collage, music, drawing, ICT, storytelling, poetry and photography.

There are pupil activity sheets to accompany some of the strategies: these are found in the online resources PDF.

Sources of stories, images and films are found on the inside back cover.

CREATE

Useful for

Getting young pupils to be observant and ask good questions.

See also

Trading places–3
Rumour mill–74
Mystery bag–83
Questioning images–87

19 Paintbox

Strategy

- Give pupils a photograph or image, e.g. the inside of a synagogue (Judaism); a Nativity scene (Christianity); the Guru Granth Sahib being read in a gurdwara (Sikhism).
- Ask pupils to concentrate closely and then list four colours in the picture. They should put them in order – from the colour shown most often to the colour shown least often. They might do this by creating a colour chart that the artist/designer had used, showing the colours used most often as a larger block of colour.
- Get pupils to compare their ideas about colours with another pupil who has worked on the same – or a different – picture. Ask pupils: Why did the artist or the designer (of a building, for example) use these colours? What is the importance of these colours? What difference would it make if different colours had been used? Are the colours symbolic? What do they mean?

Useful for

Exploring issues which can be expressed in terms of a continuum between two opposites, e.g. good and evil; peace and war; love and hate; justice and injustice.

See also

Human barchart–16
Natural collage–23
Yes or no–55

20 Collage

Strategy

- Provide pupils with newspapers, colour supplements, magazines and glue, and ask them to produce a collage of a given theme, e.g. evil, crucifixion, love. Scissors are not always required as the act of tearing can be part of the process, and the rough edges symbolic.

Example: Good and evil collage

- Put pupils in groups. Explain that one corner of the paper represents evil and the opposite corner represents good. The group then work together to create a collage depicting a continuum or journey from the negative to the positive, using pictures, colours, symbols, words torn or cut out of magazines and newspapers. The images express the group's ideas, feelings and questions about the issues; these can be shared with other groups or the whole class. Ask pupils to write in fewer than 50 words: What does it express? What works well?

Useful for

Exploring how music can express inner feelings and beliefs.

See also

Making music–33
Observation–23
Feelings graph–96

21 Music

Strategy

- Arrange the class in small groups of 4–5. Play several different types of music (contemporary and classical) that express spiritual or religious feelings, stories, beliefs or celebrations. Ask pupils to suggest some. Links to a wide collection of examples are found on NATRE's website (www.natre.org.uk) – 'Developing RE through music'.
- Following each piece of music, ask the groups to share ideas about: (a) Why were the music and/or lyrics written? (b) How might the composer have been feeling at the time? (c) What did the composer want to convey? Feed ideas back to the class.
- Hold a group discussion about how music is used in society today and, in particular, in religion.
- Ask pupils to suggest any genres of religious music they know, for example hymns praise songs; kirtans (Sikhism); nasheeds (Islam); spirituals; classical pieces (e.g. Handel's Messiah); rock worship; songs for life's milestones such as weddings and funerals.

22 In the gallery

Strategy

- Give pupils a photograph or image, e.g. a baby being baptised (Christianity); the aqiqah ceremony (Islam); a family celebrating Hanukkah (Judaism); worship at the gurdwara (Sikhism).

- Ask pupils to imagine that the picture is being displayed in a gallery. In pairs, they must come up with:
  - a title for the picture. It needs to help people looking at the picture know what it is about; it also needs to be interesting, and to make people want to look.
  - the entry for a gallery catalogue. This needs to give some information about the work of art and some questions to think about.

Useful for

Developing visual learning; encouraging questioning and talking about aspects of religious life.

See also

23 Natural collage

Strategy

- Provide each individual pupil, or each small group, with something natural like a flower on a stem with leaves attached, or a twig with leaves. Or ask them to collect natural objects from the school grounds. Also provide them with a selection of quotations from religious and non-sacred texts reflecting the chosen theme.

- Introduce a theme such as change, death and rebirth, or brokenness in human relationships. Ask pupils to use the natural things they have been given to express the feelings and understandings they connect with the theme they have been given. They should also use some of the quotations from sacred texts to support their explanation or make links between their image and the ideas in the texts.

Useful for

Encouraging reflection and imaginative and creative expression of human experiences; stimulating discussion.

See also

24 Masks

Strategy

- Introduce pupils to a story from a faith tradition, e.g. by reading it to them or showing them a film version. Ask them to identify: key characters; the type of roles they play in the story; the main emotions each character is associated with; the turning points in the story; how the identity of the characters is shown.

- Pupils create masks for the main characters and use them to act out the story. They might also devise a prequel and/or a sequel to the story they are studying.

- Examples might include Krishna Steals the Butter (Hinduism); Peter during Holy Week (Christianity); Abraham and Isaac (Judaism).

Useful for

Engaging interest; retelling faith stories; interpretation and visual expression of concepts such as good and evil; exploring identity and how it is hidden or revealed.

See also

25 Drawing around

Useful for

Getting young pupils to look closely at a picture and interpret/suggest meaning.

See also

Look, talk and draw—27

Rumour mill—74

Pictures from memory—93

Online resources PDF

Strategy

- Show pupils a picture, but with a part of it hidden. Choose a picture which has something surprising and unexpected in the part you will reveal last, e.g. The Feeding of the 5000 (Christianity) – show first just Jesus; a mother showing her children how the challah bread is prepared at Shabbat (Judaism) – show first just the mother; men sweeping the road ahead of the lorry carrying the Guru Granth Sahib in procession at Baisakhi (Sikhism) – show first just the men.

- There are various ways of working with the picture, e.g.:
  - give pupils half of a picture and ask them to draw what they think the other half of the picture will be like
  - give pupils the central part of a picture and ask them to draw what they think will be around it
  - give pupils a smaller part of the picture, e.g. a quarter. If it is a piece of artwork based on a story, give pupils the story too, so that they can work out from that what the rest of the picture might look like. They can then compare their ideas with the artist's.

26 Simulation

Useful for

Encouraging observation, thought and reflection; engaging with a member of a faith community.

See also

Digital storytelling—31

Visitors—46 & 47

Pictures from memory—93

Strategy

- Set up in the classroom a simulation of an aspect of religious life, such as a Buddhist or Hindu shrine used for worship, using the appropriate artefacts. Handling Hindu murti statues in the classroom is acceptable if these are not consecrated; images of the Buddha are fine too.

- Invite a member of the relevant faith community into the classroom to speak about his/her faith and particularly about the aspect that is the subject of the simulation. Encourage pupils to look carefully at the simulation, listen to the visitor speaking and then write a short poem or a piece of prose explaining their own attitudes to and questions about the main focus (e.g. worship). Ask them to label a diagram of the simulation – but with emotions and beliefs rather than naming parts.

27 Look, talk and draw

Useful for

Using and developing young pupils' skills such as visual memory, observation, descriptive language, co-operation and teamwork.

See also

Keyhole movie—29

Rumour mill—74

Mystery bag—83

Through the keyhole—88

Strategy

- Arrange pupils in fours and name them Pair A and Pair B. Give a simple picture to Pair A (e.g. baptism candle) and let them look at it for one or two minutes, and then take the picture away.

- Pair A describe the picture to Pair B, and then have to stop talking while Pair B try to draw the picture. After a few minutes, you can allow Pair B to ask Pair A one question. Allow Pair B to look at the picture and talk with Pair A about how close they got to drawing it. As pupils get used to this kind of activity you can use more detailed images.

28 Create a cover

Strategy

- Ask pupils which image they would use on the cover of a book (or film DVD cover or music CD) about, for example, a religion pupils are studying, celebrations, special places, happiness, love, God, peace or stories from a sacred text.
- Ask them – what if the book was for older pupils? Or younger pupils? Ask them to draw their ideas if there is not a good enough image in the pictures you show them. What would they call the book?
- With older pupils you might ask them to write a 50-word 'blurb' or 'quote' for the back cover, to explain what is in the book and to encourage people to read it.

Useful for

Synthesising and applying learning; consolidating learning.

See also

29 Keyhole movie

Strategy

- Identify a movie clip that shows an aspect of religious life, e.g. preparing the Guru Granth Sahib for its nightly rest (Sikhism); waking the gods in the mandir (Hinduism). You will need the keyhole or spotlight tool on a whiteboard. Good clips for RE can be found on www.cleo.net.uk and www.bbc.co.uk/learningzone/clips.
- Explain to pupils that they are looking at a 'keyhole view' into a place that is special to someone. Ask them to suggest whom it is special to and why. Slowly move the 'keyhole' around the screen, inviting pupils to suggest ideas. Ask them what they can see and hear. How does the movie make them feel? What might it remind them of? What do the colours and shapes tell them?
- When the movie has been identified, ask pupils what they think will happen next. What else do they need to find out to help them understand what is so special about the place? Where can they look to find out? And finally, what three questions would they want to ask?

Useful for

Encouraging focus on detail to interpret/ infer meaning; providing stimulus to a challenging question; preparing pupils for a visit or to receive visitors.

See also

30 Photoboard

Strategy

- Provide pupils with a collection of photographs or images taken from magazines or websites, some glue and marker pens. Ask them to select from the images those that can be sequenced together to tell the story of a moral dilemma. They should add speech bubbles to the characters to show the nature of the dilemma, the responses of the character, the final outcome and comment from at least one of the characters about how they feel.
- Dilemmas might include:
  - David, who is Jewish, has been picked for the school football team, but the first match is on Saturday, which is the Sabbath and he is expected to be at home with his family.
  - Ayesha, who is Muslim, has been asked to go to a school disco. Her mum says she should think about whether it will be a help to her faith or not.

Useful for

Developing discussion and evaluation skills; exploring moral decision-making.

See also

CREATE

Useful for

Bringing the authentic voice of religion into the RE classroom; providing opportunities for dialogue with people of faith; supporting collaborative work.

See also

Hotseat–27

Interviewing–74

Visitors–46 & 47

31 Digital storytelling

Strategy

- Arrange for pupils to meet with members of a local faith community either in the classroom or in their place of worship. Also arrange for pupils to have access to digital cameras to record their interviews, and facilities to edit them afterwards.

- Explain to pupils that they will work in small groups to develop a set of questions for an interview with members of a local faith community. They will choose one or two of their group to do the actual interview, while the others operate the camera equipment. They will then all work together to create a digital presentation telling the 'story' that was shared with them.

- Pupils present their digital story to the class; they could take part in a recorded hotseating activity to support assessment.

Useful for

Conveying complex ideas using a visual vocabulary familiar to the pupils.

See also

Board games–67

Through the keyhole–88

32 Timemorph

Strategy

- Create a morph sequence of two or more images using appropriate software. For example, a photograph of a place of worship taken 50 years ago and a photograph of the same place of worship, taken from exactly the same position and angle today (for an example see: www. cleo.net.uk).

- As pupils watch the morph sequence ask them to:

  - Work in pairs to note down the differences they observe

  - Move into fours to share/add/amend ideas and then feedback to the class

  - Work in fours to categorise the key points into the following groups: building; worship; people; feelings

  - Identify the reasons for the changes they observe

  - Identify three things they want to investigate when they visit a local place of worship

  - Identify three questions they would like to ask the religious leader of the place they visit.

Useful for

Finding out if pupils understand the context, use and purpose of religious artefacts or pictures; getting pupils to talk about their understanding of religious artefacts.

See also

Drawing around–25

Mystery bag–83

Pictures from memory–93

Online resources PDF

33 Picture extending

Strategy

- Give pupils a copy of a picture, or an artefact, and ask them to finish it. Encourage pupils to think about:

  - The setting they would normally expect to see the picture or object in

  - Other pictures/objects they associate with it which might also need to shown

  - Colours and symbols they associate with the picture/object (and what these may mean).

- Pupils either write or give a brief verbal commentary on their picture

34 Senses poems

Strategy

- Helping pupils to focus on a video clip, with a purpose for watching; enabling pupils to evaluate the most significant elements of a video clip, and express their ideas thoughtfully.
- Identify a stimulus for the activity. Film clips are perhaps most suitable for the classroom.
- Put pupils in groups of five, numbering them 1–5. As they watch the film clip, ask them to focus on what they see (Pupil 1), hear (Pupil 2), touch (Pupil 3), taste (Pupil 4) and smell (Pupil 5).
- Then gather all the 1s together, all the 2s together, and so on, to talk about what they saw.
- Pupils move back into mixed groups of 1–5s to write lines of their poem. Using the sentence starters below, Pupil 1 completes the sentence about what s/he 'saw', and others follow suit, completing the line of the poem they have focused on, choosing what struck them most, or that they consider the most important response.
- As a group, pupils then complete the sentence starters below together, discussing their ideas. A template is available in the online resources PDF.
- Finally, the lines are merged to form a poem, as in the example given here.

Useful for
Synthesising and applying learning; consolidating learning.

See also

Talking circle–100
Different audiences–116
Online resources PDF

Senses poem: example

I saw the face of man, the confusion and chaos
  I noticed the face of the divine
I heard the blaring of the horns, the cheers of 1000 throats and the clapping of the hands
  I wanted to say the mantras of 1000 voices
I touched the elements of earth, water, flowers, my family, my friends, my fellow humans
  I felt the sacredness of the goddess
I tasted mud and sweat
  It reminded me of sweetness and joy
I could smell the stench of 1000 bodies
  It was like incense floating to heaven
I wondered why so many, why now, why am I here?
  It made me ask, why?

I saw …	I noticed …
I heard …	I wanted to say …
I touched …	I felt …
I tasted …	It reminded me of …
I could smell …	It was like …
I wondered …	It made me think about …

Photocopy permission

CREATE

Useful for

Encouraging pupils to look carefully, question, analyse, reflect and interpret the meaning and significance of images.

See also

Rumour mill–74

Questioning images–87

35 Photographs and pictures

Strategy

- Provide pupils, either in small groups or as a whole class, with a photograph or picture of sufficient size for them to see details clearly; it could be displayed on an IWB.
- Ask pupils to study the photograph or picture very closely and to ask questions of those in the picture exploring actions, motives, objects, symbols and relationships. For example, pupils could ask (depending on the picture):
  - What can you see in the picture?
  - Is there a story behind the picture? What is it?
  - What are the people doing? Why?
  - What might they be saying?
  - Have you ever seen anything like this before? What is it like?
  - Can you see all the people who have shared in planning or running this event, or are some of them outside the picture?
  - What would happen if one person suddenly stopped taking part or wasn't there?
  - How do you think each person is feeling? Have you ever felt like that?

Example for younger pupils

- Display a collection of Christmas cards with specifically Christian images on a board or large sheet. Pupils then write questions around them for others to answer.

Example for older pupils

- Display a religious image from an online art gallery, or one that shows the consequences of a natural disaster.

Useful for

Expressing understanding of religious symbolism or the meaning of a faith story.

See also

RE-enactment–7

Music–21

36 Making music

Strategy

- Show pupils a religious artefact or tell them a faith story and ask them to use a range of musical instruments to express their understanding of the meaning and symbolism. Percussion and body music, rhythm and chant, clapping and stamping, humming or whistling can all be excellent.
- Examples might include: the Seder Plate (Judaism): a statue of Shiva (Hinduism); a crucifix (Christianity); the Parable of the Lost Son (Christianity); the story of Guru Nanak Lost in the River (Sikhism); Queen Maya's Dream (Buddhism).
- Alternatively they could make up a song to retell a faith story and sing it to a familiar tune, or write and perform a rap on a spiritual or moral theme.

Useful for

Displaying understanding of concepts and ideas; supporting self-expression and communication.

See also

Post-it®'s–54

Wall of wisdom–56

37 Banners

Strategy

- Ask pupils to produce a banner to capture the essence of an issue they have been studying, e.g. about freedom after studying Pesach (Judaism); about trade justice after studying the work of Christian Aid or CAFOD (Christianity); about equality after studying Islamophobia (Islam).
- Features of a good banner: wide but not tall; simple, witty words; a single powerful image that communicates instantly.

© RE Today Services 2013

ENQUIRE

Enquiring RE begins with young children: their first skills as enquirers come from exercising curiosity and pursuing the will to discover. This leads to increasingly sophisticated research, in which pupils investigate for themselves, set their own agendas for learning and become researchers in simple ways.

In this section you will find a wide variety of strategies that provide pupils with opportunities to develop their ideas, understandings and questions in RE through enquiry, for example through asking good questions, interviewing visitors, solving mysteries, analysing problems, speculating and taking the role of envoy.

There are pupil activity sheets to accompany some of the strategies; these are found on the online resources PDF.

Sources of stories, images and films are found on the inside back cover.

ENQUIRE

Useful for

Encouraging young pupils to speculate and ask good questions.

See also

Questions for the Being who knows everything—41

Mystery bag—83

38 Puzzling questions

Strategy

- Choose an intriguing object relevant to the topic you are teaching and place it in a fabric bag or a sealed cardboard box. Examples: Christianity – Easter (a wooden egg, an interesting stone or piece of wood, a plant bulb); Judaism – Shabbat (a Havdalah candle, a challah loaf, a silver goblet); Islam – prayer (subha (prayer beads), prayer mat, compass).
- Ask pupils 'What do you think I have got in here?' Encourage them to guess. Play 'Twenty Questions' – pupils can ask questions and the teacher may only answer yes or no.
- Talk about what it is like when you don't know something you really want to know. How does it feel? What might you do to find the answer?
- Reveal what is in the box. Ask pupils questions like: How do you feel now the mystery is solved? What new questions does the object raise? How can you find the answers? Ask pupils to decide which are the best questions asked by the class.
- Tell pupils that you will be getting them to ask lots of questions about the world during RE and other subjects. Consider collecting them in a big 'Why?' book.

Useful for

Encouraging pupils to ask and respond to deeper questions.

See also

Good questions, better questions—44

Enquiring into religious practice—48

Ultimate questions—92

39 Question box

Strategy

- Ask each pupil to prepare a question on a given subject. Collect all the questions and put them in a box. Redistribute the questions to other pupils for them to discover the answer.
- For younger pupils: What makes a hero? What would you like to ask Jesus, Muhammad or Moses? What would you like to ask someone featured in a video (e.g. a Hindu worshipping at a home shrine; a Muslim on Hajj)? What would you like to ask God? What puzzles you about life and death?
- For older pupils: What happens when we die? If God exists, why does he allow innocent people to suffer? What is the relationship between religion and science? What arguments are there for and against the existence of God? Is it ever right to have an abortion? Can war ever be justified?

Useful for

Enhancing linguistic competence; developing critical thinking skills.

See also

Visitors—46 & 47

Zebra—91

Socratic questioning—115

40 Probing questions

Strategy

- Ask pupils a challenging question – let them research and debate it, and present the outcomes to the class. For example:
  - What is more important: love or freedom?
  - How do we know that the world is how we experience it?
  - If some people say there is a God, and others say there isn't, who is right and how?
  - What is a good human being? What do you mean by 'good'?
  - Could God make an unbreakable cup? If he did, could he break it?

41 Questions for the Being who knows everything

Strategy

- Ask pupils to think/pair/share and come up with the questions they would like to ask the Being who knows everything if s/he came to their RE lesson. Explain that for many religious people, it is God who knows everything.

- Record the questions on the whiteboard or ask pupils to write them on sticky notes. Pupils then choose three of the questions and have a go at answering them.

- Questions and answers can be used as a stimulus for further class discussion. They can also be used to provide a matching activity (match the question with an appropriate answer) or added to a class 'Why?' book.

- As an alternative, offer pupils a selection of answers from religious believers. Which do they think are the most persuasive or compelling? Are there some questions about mysteries that we will never be able to explain? Video clips of young people from a variety of faiths giving their questions for God can be found on NATRE's 'Listening to children and young people talking' database – www.natre.org.uk/db.

Useful for
Encouraging pupils to ask and respond to big questions.

See also

Puzzling questions–38
Question box–39
Ultimate questions–92

42 Envoys

Strategy

- After group work has been completed, one person is chosen to be an 'envoy'. The envoy moves to a new group to explain and summarise the findings of the first group and to find out what the new group thought, decided or achieved.

- The envoy returns to the original group and reports back.

Useful for
Sharing what has been discovered and learned during group work without whole-class feedback.

See also

Post-its®–54
Wall of wisdom–56
Snowballing–77

43 Interviewing

Strategy

- Decide the issue that is to be explored, e.g. Why should Christians (or Muslims, Hindus, etc) care about people who are poor, hungry or badly treated? Should euthanasia be legalised?

- Divide the class into two – one half are to be the interviewers, and the other the interviewees. Give pupils time before the activity for interviewers to devise questions to ask about the chosen issue, and interviewees to research the issue and work out their opinion on it. This can be done in class or homework time.

- Pair an interviewer with an interviewee. The interviewer asks her/his questions, and gets responses, making a short recording. Interviewers analyse the responses, synthesise the information and summarise the opinions of the interviewees.

- Interviewees meet together in groups to share their findings on the issue, clarify their opinions, identify similarities and differences of opinion. Interviewers report back to the rest of the class.

Useful for
Researching moral, social and religious issues; developing speaking, listening, evaluating and social skills.

See also

Hotseat–17
Visitors–46 & 47
Reflection alley–53

ENQUIRE

Encouraging pupils to raise and engage with puzzling questions; encouraging pupils to respond to questions with some answers of their own, and consider other answers.

See also

Persona dolls–15

Debate–81

Socratic questioning–115

Online resources PDF

44 Good questions, better questions

Strategy

- Give pupils a page of 40+ questions on a given topic. An example of 40+ questions focusing on Islam is provided in the online resources PDF, e.g. Why do Muslims want to remember the Prophet Muhammad? What do Muslims think about Jesus? Why do Muslims like to visit Makkah, and what do they do there? Why do some people think Islam is to do with terrorism?
- Ask pupils to work in twos or threes to do the following five things with the questions:
  - Read the questions aloud to each other and say if each one is simple, complex, mysterious, intriguing, and say why.
  - Attack the page with a marker pen, crossing out 30 of the questions – all the ones they don't want to answer. Ask pupils to remember to include some that they think are difficult – or even impossible – to answer.
  - Work alone for a few minutes on one of the questions (possibly one given by another member of the group). How could they find the answer? Ask pupils to create a five-point 'research plan' to find out the answer to their questions. Whom could they ask? What breakdown of the question into smaller chunks could they make? Are there several possible answers? What research do they need to do?
  - Share their research plans with the rest of the group.
  - Suggest a few more questions that they think should be added to the original list of 40+.
- Collect the questions in which pupils have shown an interest, and follow up the ideas they have. Come back to the next lesson with video clips, online searches, interview possibilities and all kinds of starting points for curious pupils to pursue their own investigations.

45 Analysing questions

Analysing and evaluating questions; identifying good enquiry questions; discerning the difference between factual questions and those that depend upon interpretation.

See also

Good questions, better questions–44

Buttresses–114

Strategy

- Ask pupils to identify a list of questions arising out of the topic they are studying. Ask them to sort the questions into four categories as follows:

  Questions which have only one right answer:
  - Which ones are about understanding the facts? (**comprehension**)
  - Which ones would need some specialist knowledge? (**knowledge**)

  Questions which have many possible answers:
  - Which ones use your imagination? (**speculation**)
  - Which ones open up a good enquiry? (**enquiry**)
- Groups of pupils then choose a question from each of the four categories and are given some time and resources to answer them. Which questions were the most difficult to answer?

46 Visitors: for pupils

Strategy

- Explain the proposed lesson and its purpose – interviewing a visitor (e.g. a local minister, charity worker, imam, MP).

- Stress the importance of asking questions and listening to answers. Remind pupils of the ground rules for good behaviour.

- Ask pupils to think about whether their questions are 'open', 'closed' or 'loaded', and whether they could be offensive or invade the visitor's privacy. Pupils apply the analysis of questions outlined in Strategy 45.

- Get groups of four pupils to generate four sensible questions to put to the visitor, drawing on their background work in RE.

- Choose or elect two or three pupils to meet, greet and introduce the visitor. Choose pupils to give a vote of thanks and accompany the visitor to reception after the lesson. Provide opportunity for these pupils to rehearse these functions and jobs.

Useful for

Generating and posing open-ended questions; developing speaking and listening skills; developing sensitivity and empathy; practising the courtesies of greeting, introducing and thanking.

See also

Visitors–47
Digital storytelling–31
Interviewing–43

47 Visitors: for visitors

Strategy

- Establish that the visitor you have in mind is effective in the classroom; consider asking colleagues in other schools you know if they have had a good experience with that visitor.

- Ask the visitor to bring three or more artefacts or a bag of interesting objects to 'show and share'. This helps get the level of discussion right for the pupils.

- Make sure the visitor:
  - understands the context of the visit and the amount of time available
  - is told the age and ability of the pupils and the topic they are working on
  - is aware of any important background information s/he needs, especially if dealing with personally sensitive issues
  - discusses with you how s/he wishes to use the session
  - is advised about what to expect in terms of pupil response and participation.

- Remember that visitors can be used in a variety of ways. Consider the learning needs of the class as well as the preference of the visitor. For example:
  - with small groups of pupils who have the responsibility for preparing an agenda and then the opportunity to practise social skills and learn about the chosen topic
  - with the whole class
  - in a *Question Time* or panel format as a visiting expert prepared to answer questions from the audience.

Useful for

Generating the right atmosphere; making best use of the visitor's time.

See also

Keyhole movie–29
Digital storytelling–31
Visitors–46

ENQUIRE

Useful for

Understanding the connection between what people believe and what they do.

See also

Simulation–26

Digital storytelling–31

Similarities and differences–90

48 Enquiring into religious practice

Strategy

- Provide pupils with four pictures of regular practice in the religion you are studying. For example, for Sikhism: people listening to the Guru Granth Sahib being read; praying; singing kirtan accompanied by musical instruments; sharing food in the langar. Stick each picture in the centre of a sheet of A3 paper.

- Arrange pupils in four groups and give each group one of the A3 sheets. The sheets are then moved in a carousel round the class, with each group doing the next activity on the list with the sheet they have just received. Ask pupils to:

  - Write any questions they have about the picture they have been given. Allow about two minutes for this. Pass the paper to the next group.

  - Add in any further questions and answer any questions posed by the first group. Allow about five minutes for this. Pass the paper to the next group.

  - Research in books or on the internet to clarify what is happening in the picture and then as a group write a paragraph which could be displayed next to the picture to explain what is happening. Allow about 30 minutes. Pass the paper to the next group.

  - Receive the finished work and read it through. Add corrections, amendments and any additional ideas. Choose two people in your picture and draw a thought cloud. Write what they may be thinking.

- Groups share their finished picture with the whole class. What has been learned about religious practice in the religion studied? What questions still remain?

Useful for

Sorting relevant from irrelevant information; interpreting information; making links between disparate bits of information; speculating to form a hypothesis; checking, refining and explaining; getting pupils talking about their actual learning and thinking processes.

See also

Similarities and differences–90

Fact or opinion–102

Online resources PDF

49 Mysteries

Strategy

- Arrange pupils in groups of four and give them a central question to answer or a problem to solve, such as 'Why did …. happen?' See the example on the next page and in the online resources PDF.

- Provide pupils with a series of clues which they have to sort through, make sense of, agree on and produce a plausible (not absolute) answer to the question or mystery. It is useful to cut the clues up and put them in envelopes for each group with the key question on the front. Try to provide some additional visual clues to the mystery, e.g. maps, photographs, diagrams or letters.

- Encourage pupils to look together at each clue in turn, ask questions and offer reasons for any suggestions they make. The aim is for the group to agree on a plausible solution to the question or mystery, with reasons for their conclusions.

- Ask pupils to feed back to the class their answer, with a full explanation.

- Talk with the class about how they did the activity. Prompt them with questions like 'What did you do with the cards first?' and 'Why?' to get the discussion started. This will help pupils become explicitly aware of problem-solving strategies that can be more widely applied.

Mystery: Will Amir go on Hajj next year?

Amir is 15 in April next year.	Makkah is in Saudi Arabia.	Amir is hoping to do A levels and go on to university.	Amir is scared of flying.
Amir is a Muslim. His father is an imam (a leader at a mosque) in Gloucester.	Muslims have to perform the Five Pillars of Islam.	Pilgrims must wear white as a sign of unity and equality.	Amir is diabetic.
The 'Pillars' include declaring Shahadah, praying five times daily, fasting during the month of Ramadan, and giving money to the poor.	In the centre of the Haram Mosque in Makkah is the Ka'ba – the temple first built by Adam (pbuh) for the worship of Allah.	Hajj is a once in a lifetime pilgrimage to Makkah.	The Ka'ba is the closest place to heaven. It is the holiest place on earth.
Amir's grandfather died last year without having been on Hajj. He and Amir were very close.	Many Muslims believe that Allah will answer all prayers offered while on Hajj.	The Fifth Pillar is Hajj. All Muslims should go on Hajj at least once in their lifetime if they are able to.	Offering Hajj in a right spirit can mean that a pilgrim (or hajji) will get into heaven.
Makkah is the birthplace of Muhammad (pbuh).	Amir is a cricket fan. England have an away series against Pakistan in January next year.	Pilgrims on Hajj follow in the footsteps of Muhammad (pbuh) in his last journey to Makkah.	It is permitted to do Hajj on someone else's behalf, if they are too ill or if they have died.
Hajj takes place over a five-day period. This year it was in mid-January. Next year it will be early January.	Hajj celebrates the Muslim *ummah* or community. Three million Muslims from all over the world worship together.	Amir studies the Qur'an at madrassah (mosque school) most evenings.	Amir's family is not having a summer holiday this year.

Photocopy permission

ENQUIRE

Useful for

Encouraging young pupils to think about and reflect on what matters in a religious story.

See also

Freeze-frame–5
Pictures from memory–93

50 What really matters?

Strategy

- Tell pupils a religious story. The Christian story of Holy Week and Easter is used in this example, but the activities can be easily adapted to stories in other religious traditions.

- Set up a table or tray with 10 items associated with Holy Week and Easter (e.g. a hot cross bun, a chocolate egg, a cuddly toy rabbit, a daffodil, a palm cross, a crucifix and an empty cross, an Easter card, a glass of wine and a toy plastic donkey).

- Play 'Kim's Game'. Ask pupils to look at the tray, then cover it and ask them if they can remember all ten things on the tray. Ask one pupil to suggest two of the objects that belong together and say why. Give several pupils the chance to do this, and accept all answers.

- Ask pupils if they can say what each object has to do with the stories of Jesus that they have heard. If no one can connect one of the objects, then fill in more detail. Use talk time to reinforce details of the story and remind the group of key points.

- Discuss with pupils whether you can have Easter without these things. Talk about the different answers – there is no right or wrong.

- Invite pupils to choose three of the objects that they think are the best reminders of the story. Which of the objects might matter most to a Christian, or might help them remember Jesus' story?

- Ask pupils to use a paper template (e.g. a big circle divided into three) and make three drawings of the things that matter most at Easter. In small groups, pupils speak and listen about their work.

- Encourage pupils to make some links between the things that matter to Christians at Holy Week and Easter and the things, people and questions that matter most to them.

Useful for

Encouraging active participation in expressing insights and identifying a resolution to a problem; analysing religious and non-religious responses to a problem.

See also

Analysing questions–45
Mysteries–45
Agenda-setting–82

51 Analysing a problem

Strategy

- Put pupils into discussion groups and identify the problem they are to discuss. Provide some stimulus so that all pupils have some background information, such as a newspaper article, online news clip, short film clip. Include some guidance from sacred texts that might be used in the decision-making process.

- Pupils suggest responses to the following questions, which provide a framework for their discussion and for action planning:
  - What is the problem?
  - Whom does it affect?
  - Where, when and why does it happen?
  - How could it be tackled?
  - What is the best way forward?
  - Who will take action?
  - How will the action be monitored and reviewed?

- Problems tackled might include: a concern about racial prejudice in the local community; an increase in the number of food banks being opened in the area.

REFLECT

The skills of reflection include noticing, listening and attentiveness, and there is a dual focus in reflective work, on both the self and the stimulus for learning. In good reflective RE, pupils engage with religious and spiritual materials for themselves and respond with their own increasing insights.

In this section you will find a wide variety of strategies that provide pupils with opportunities to develop their ideas, understandings and questions in RE in a reflective and thoughtful way, for example through guided story, RE board games, visual learning, discussion, guided story, values clarification and brainstorming.

There are pupil activity sheets to accompany some of the strategies; these are found in the online resources PDF.

Sources of stories, images and films are found on the inside back cover.

REFLECT

Useful for

Encouraging visual learning in younger pupils; encouraging empathy and speculation to deepen learning.

See also

Paintbox–19

In the gallery–22

Drawing around–25

Online resources PDF

52 Bubbling speech . . . bubbling thoughts

Strategy

- Show pupils a pair of images with something in common, either printed or displayed on the whiteboard, e.g. a girl reading a children's Bible and a priest reading a Bible in a church service (Christianity); a boy reading the Torah (Judaism) and a boy reading the Qur'an (Islam); parents watching their baby being baptised (Christianity) and a father whispering the call to prayer in the ear of his newborn child (Islam).

- Give pupils some blank *speech* bubbles (or ask them to draw their own). Ask them to imagine what the people in the pictures might be saying. They may record these in writing or simply use the bubbles to help them think and talk themselves. There is a template in the online resources PDF.

- Then give out some blank *thought* bubbles. We don't always say what we are thinking, so ask pupils to reflect on what the people in the pictures might be thinking. There is a template in the online resources PDF.

- Share some information/quotations from faith representatives to give some insiders' responses – what are *they* saying/thinking?

53 Reflection alley

Strategy

Useful for

Expressing own viewpoint in relation to others' views, using reason and argument; evaluating the significance of a range of views and coming to a well-argued conclusion.

See also

Human barchart–16

XY grid–57

Balloon debate–79

Buttresses–114

- Set up the classroom so that at the front there are two parallel rows of seats, sufficient for five or six pupils in each row, with an alleyway between them so that one pupil (the 'walker') can walk between then. The rest of the class is seated as an audience so that they can see the 'walker'.

- Present the class with a dilemma arising out of their studies, e.g. What should the soldier who was ordered to crucify Jesus do? Can a case be made for euthanasia? Is violent protest ever justified? Decide as a class what the possible courses of action or opinions are, suggesting reasons and evidence for their ideas.

- Choose a volunteer to 'face the dilemma' by walking up reflection alley.

- Ask 10–12 pupils to join in the reflection alley as advisers. Pupils on one side of the alley should offer advice on one course of action, and on the other side to give reasons for another course of action.

- The walk is done as a performance for the rest of the class. The walker begins by describing the question, then asks the pupils on either side, 'What should I do?' – first one on the left, then one on the right, and so on.

- The walker can ask supplementary questions and have a dialogue with each person. At the end of the walk, the walker has half a minute in silence, and then says what decision she or he would make and why.

54 Post-it®s
Strategy

- At a significant point in a lesson, or sequence of lessons, provide pupils with Post-it® notes and ask them to make a personal response to a question, story or picture to reflect their understanding and any questions they have. If a picture is used, it can be put in the centre of the space being used, with Post-it®s placed around it.
- Post-it®s can be stuck on the wall or on a large sheet of paper and provide a stimulus to discussion. Similar responses can be grouped to reflect the main ideas expressed by the class. Questions raised can be addressed subsequently to support learning.
- Repeat the activity at a later point in a lesson or series of lessons to identify development in understanding and/or changes in opinions; the reasons for change can be the focus of ongoing discussion.

Useful for

Consolidating learning; stimulating reflection and empathy; encouraging involvement of all.

See also

News bulletins–6
Banners–37

55 Yes or no
Strategy

- Devise a list of questions about a topic or belief pupils are studying to which the answer is either yes or no, right or wrong, true or false. Questions can be asked of pupils in turn, or answers requested of the class by a show of hands.
- Alternatively pupils, in groups of three or four, can devise their own questions on an aspect of a given topic or belief which require answers of either yes or no, right or wrong, true or false. They then 'test' another group in the class, who, in turn, test them on a different aspect.
- For example, on the theme of the Sikh celebration of Baisakhi, groups in the class could be given these aspects: the founding of the Khalsa; the life of Guru Gobind Singh; the amrit ceremony; how Baisakhi is celebrated today.

Useful for

Assessing factual knowledge and simple understanding.

See also

Timemorph–32
Yardstick–89
Fact or opinion–102

56 Wall of wisdom
Strategy

- At the end of a lesson or unit of work, provide pupils with opportunity to consider and record their observations, questions and insights arising from their studies. These can be written on paper or card and displayed on a physical wall, for example a noticeboard. They could also be written electronically and displayed in a dedicated space on the school network.
- Give opportunity for pupils to add to their responses, and to comment on those written by others.

Useful for

Consolidating, celebrating and extending learning; recognising pupils' achievement and insight; provoking discussion.

See also

Newsboards–70
Yo-yo–75
Just a minute–85

REFLECT

Developing discussion and evaluation skills; encouraging expression of personal viewpoints; enabling pupils to recognise a range of viewpoints, and see that there is diversity of belief within and between faiths.

See also

Human barchart–16
Snowflake–80
Debate–81
Online resources PDF

57 X Y grid

Strategy

- Draw an x and y axis grid on the whiteboard or on individual sheets for small groups of pupils to work on. Label the axes with four perspectives on the given issue: e.g. if considering interpretations of the biblical book of Genesis, label the x axis as 'sees Genesis story as literal' at one end and 'sees Genesis story as metaphorical' at the other. Label the y axis as 'writer believes the Genesis story' at one end and 'writer does not believe the story' at the other. A template is available in the online resources PDF.

- Provide a set of statements about the chosen topic for each group of pupils and ask them to place them on the point of the grid where they think they fit. As they place the quotations, pupils talk about the views expressed and how far they agree or disagree with them.

- Examples of statements for interpretations of Genesis might include:

  - God created the world in seven days just as it says in Genesis. Science is wrong.

  - The narrative in Genesis is true but not literally true: it contains truths about what God is like.

  - The Genesis narrative is nonsense: how could light come before the sun?

  - This is a great poem and describes what some people think about God, but I still think God is imaginary.

  - I believe God created the world from nothing, but not in seven days. This poem shows God's power not his methods.

- A template and set of questions for the topic 'Views of hell' are included in the online resources PDF.

Developing the ability to 'see' with insight, awareness and appreciation; encouraging spiritual development.

See also

Natural collage–23
Board games–67
Values auction–96

58 Observation

Strategy

- Ask pupils to observe closely their own hands (or face or eyes in a mirror, or a partner's eyes). Ask them to compare fingerprints, line patterns on the palm of the hand, the shades of colour and shape in different people's eyes. They consider how each person is unique and special. Pupils could consider what they like and don't like about themselves, what they can and cannot change, what they're good at, what skills their hands can perform, and how their hands can help others.

- Enable pupils to experience close observation of nature such as minibeasts, spiders' webs, plants or tree bark from the school grounds – or frost, icicles, ice or snow. Ask pupils:

  - What did you notice for the first time?

  - What did your careful looking make you think about?

  - What did you feel?

- Give pupils the opportunity to record their insights, thoughts and feelings creatively in words or artwork.

- Compare this way of focusing with religious beliefs and practices, such as Buddhist mindfulness meditation, or Christian Lectio Divina. How do believers see the world?

59 Stilling – learning to sit still

Strategy

Useful for

Fostering empathy and deeper self-awareness; enabling pupils to discover their own inner experience and, as a result, become more able to respect it in others.

 See also

Stilling – breathing to relax–60
Stilling – guidelines–61
Guided visualisation–62
Guided story–63

- Sitting still, relaxing and preparing the body and mind to focus and reflect are skills that need to be learned. As much care and attention is needed here as for the lesson's main activity and follow-up. This suggestion for a stilling activity is set out as a script for the teacher to read. It can be adapted and developed according to the age and experience of the group and the time available.
  - Place your chair so that it is facing me and not touching your table…
  - Sit right back on your chair so that your back is right up against the back of the chair …
  - Put both feet on the floor …
  - Place your hands in your lap or let them lie loosely on your knees or on the table in front of you …
  - Give your shoulders a shrug to make sure you're relaxed even though you're sitting upright …
  - Now you're in an alert relaxed position.

60 Stilling – breathing to relax

Strategy

Useful for

Fostering empathy and deeper self-awareness; enabling pupils to discover their own inner experience and, as a result, become more able to respect it in others.

 See also

Stilling – learning to sit still–59
Stilling – guidelines–61
Guided visualisation–62
Guided story–63

- Sitting still, relaxing and preparing the body and mind to focus and reflect are skills that need to be learned. As much care and attention is needed here as for the lesson's main activity and follow-up. This suggestion for a stilling activity is set out as a script for the teacher to read. It can be adapted and developed according to the age and experience of the group and the time available.
  - Lead an activity to help pupils sit still, e.g. 'Stilling – learning to sit still' (no.59) and then …
  - Now you're sitting in an alert relaxed position, let your eyes close gently … (or look at the floor if you prefer) ... so as not to distract others …
  - Breathe slowly and silently (count to three) … noticing the way your breath enters and leaves your body …
  - As you breath in ... begin counting (in your mind) … each time you breathe in, count to four … one … two … three … four …
  - Each time you breathe out, count to four … one … two … three … four … and then start again …
  - If your mind wanders, bring it back gently and start from one again ...
  - (Pause for a short while, building up to perhaps a couple of minutes). As a variation, ask pupils to imagine that, as they breathe out, any tensions and worries they may have are breathed out. As they breathe in, things which are pleasant, comforting and energising are breathed in.

Strategy

Guidelines for using guided visualisation and guided story in RE.

Before

- **Negotiate ground rules.** When using guided visualisation and guided story for the first time with pupils, ask for co-operation and invite them to share responsibility for what happens.
- **Start small.** Pupils won't be able to participate in an extended activity straight away, so plan for around 10 minutes, and build on this.
- **Create the right atmosphere.** Consider the following: How should pupils be seated or placed for the chosen activity? Would it be helpful to close the blinds? Should there be music playing in the background? Would a lighted candle or flower arrangement provide a useful focal point?
- **Plan B.** Have an alternative activity ready in case things don't go according to plan.

During

- **Be confident.** Start in a clear, reassuring way, making sure that pupils know what is expected of them. Speak calmly and don't forget to allow appropriate pauses in the narrative. Welcome silence.
- **Stilling.** Begin with a stilling exercise. Initially, select from the examples in this book – see strategies 59 and 60.
- **Observing.** Allow for non-active participation. A pupil can be invited to tale the role of observer, without disturbing the others in the group.
- **Time.** Keep an eye on the time; allow plenty of time for debriefing and follow-up.
- **Finishing.** Finish by inviting pupils to rejoin the group, for example: 'When you are ready … look up (or open your eyes) … stretch if you want to … Still … be calm …'
- **Silence.** Discourage talking immediately following the activity. Let there be a short pause, a moment of silence.

After

- **Follow-up.** The follow-up activity or activities need to be planned carefully, and allow some choice either in the activity itself, or in the means by which it is expressed. A script and follow-up activity for a guided visualisation and a guided story is provided on pp.43–4.
- **Sharing.** Pupils should be given the opportunity to share their thoughts, feelings and experience in full-class discussion if they wish, but this should not be insisted on, as personally sensitive issues may have been raised through the activity.
- **Debriefing.** Follow-up discussion (paired, small group or whole class) should ensure that pupils are:
  - given adequate time to share ideas, thoughts and feelings
  - encouraged to listen carefully and sensitively to the ideas, thoughts and feelings of others
  - helped to articulate their learning through experience.

62 Guided visualisation

Strategy

Useful for

Developing understanding through use of the imagination.

See also

Stilling – learning to sit still–59

Stilling – breathing to relax–61

Stilling – guidelines–61

Guided story–63

- Choose an image or concept relevant to pupils' work in RE that you want them to explore.
- **Stilling.** Start with a stilling activity (see below). Explain to pupils that you will be asking them to use their imaginations to think about the meaning and significance of some things you will show them. They will work in twos or threes to talk about their responses and then will contribute to class discussion.

Example: What matters more than money to Sikhs?

- **Equipment.** You'll need to create a bowl that appears to contain a great deal of money (newspaper cut to the size of £10 or £20 notes concealed under one or two real ones – or get some other pupils to 'colour in' some copies. Colour photocopying notes is illegal, of course. You'll also need a bowl which is empty but has a label saying 'Living a rich life is …'.

- **The script**

  - **Use the first bowl:** Place the bowl with money in the centre of the group on a table where it is visible to everyone. Ask the group to look at it and to allow thoughts, ideas and imaginings to flow through the mind. Ask them to note their feelings and ideas. Ask pupils to imagine that the bowl of money had been won by them in a competition: what would they do?

  - **Use the second bowl:** After a few minutes (2–3 is long enough) ask children to close their eyes. Remove the first bowl and replace it with the second (empty) bowl and its label. Tell pupils again to look, and allow thoughts and associations to flow through the mind and to note their feelings and ideas. Ask them to think about how they would complete the label, 'Living a rich life is …' Again, after a few minutes, remove the bowl. Allow time for individuals to note down their ideas (images are as good as words here).

- **Questions to discuss**
  Let pupils share their responses to the following questions in twos or threes, and then follow this up by a general discussion of the interpretations, feelings and questions that the symbol raises:

  - What did the bowl of money represent to you? Try and say why.
  - What association(s) did it bring to mind?
  - What did the empty bowl represent to you? Try and say why.
  - What association(s) did it bring to mind?
  - What ideas did you have about using the money?
  - How did you complete the sentence 'Living a rich life is …'?

- **Stories**
  Read together a story of Guru Nanak in which his attitude to money is made clear, and/or some sayings from Sikh scripture about the limits of cash (see www.sikhnet.com/stories). Consider what can be learned from the Sikh's wisdom about money. Ask pupils to record their learning from Sikhism in an appropriate form.

- **Sikh teaching**
  Use these quotations to explore Sikh teaching:

  - 'Even Kings and emperors with heaps of wealth and vast dominions cannot compare with an ant filled with the love of God.'
  - 'The mouth of a poor person is the treasure chest of God.'
  - 'The true path to God lies in the service of our fellow beings.'

Engaging with a text from a faith community; identifying key teachings in a story and reflecting on what these mean in practice.

See also

Stilling – learning to sit still–59

Stilling – breathing to relax–60

Stilling - guidelines

Guided visualisation–62

Online resources PDF

63 Guided story

Strategy

- Choose a story from a faith tradition that pupils are studying.

- Start with a stilling activity (see below). Explain to pupils that you will be telling them a story from a faith tradition and asking them to visualise some of the details of the story. They will then work in pairs to identify the message of the story for people in that faith tradition today.

Example: A Muslim story about Sheikh Abdul Qadir

The script

- I want you to imagine a time long ago … in a far-off country … a village called Jilan … it's hot … dusty … bustling … you live there … with your family … you know all the streets … the houses … the people … the news … the gossip …

- As you watch … you see a man you recognise … everyone is talking about him … his neighbour keeps playing loud music every time he tries to pray … what will he do? … he looks worried … he walks up and down the street knocking on the doors … he speaks to the householder … they all shake their heads … he walks away … looking dejected … then you hear the muezzin call the Muslims of the village to prayer … the man returns home … to pray …

- Time passes … the man returns to the street … he tries another door… this time the householder looks animated … they talk … the man strides away … hurriedly … purposefully … head held high … without looking back …

- Time passes … an hour or so … you see two men in the street … the man with his neighbour … they are deep in conversation … you can't quite hear everything they say, but you hear the words … 'I'm sorry' … 'so ashamed' … 'thank you' … 'why?'… you are not clear who is speaking … it doesn't seem to matter to them …

- Time passes … several days … you hear the call to prayer once again summoning Muslims to prayer … you see the man and his neighbour walking together into the mosque to pray …

- Now I want you to leave your imaginary journey … leave the two men at prayer … remember the classroom … the chairs and tables … the wall displays and the other people … picture some of the details and then … when you are ready … look up … stretch if you want to … Still … be calm.

Follow-up activities

Pupils work in twos to:

- discuss what they think the story is about

- compare their ideas with the actual story (see accompanying PDF) and clarify their understanding of what the story is teaching

- compose a sequel to the story, for example 'One month later …'

- write alternative endings (from *) from the point of view of (a) a sceptic and (b) an atheist.

- choose the wisest piece of writing they have ever read, and identify three reasons why they chose it.

A copy of the story of Sheikh Abdul Qadir can be found in the online resources PDF.

64 Rucksack

Strategy

- Provide pupils with an outline template of a rucksack, or ask them to draw one. Present them with a situation as a result of which they have to choose items to put inside the rucksack. Three examples are given below.

Example 1: What matters most?

- Imagine that you are going on a long journey (to somewhere hot or cold, isolated or busy, for example). All you can take with you are the things that you can fit into your rucksack – the bare necessities. What would you choose to take and why? What beliefs, practices, teachings, stories, images and values might a person from a religious faith pack in his/her rucksack and why?

Example 2: People in need

- Imagine that you can put not only things but qualities into your rucksack (e.g. kindness, friendship, courage). Think and talk about:
  - The qualities you would like to demonstrate or take with you on your journey through life
  - The sorts of things we sometimes carry around with is that we would be better off leaving behind (e.g. grudges, regrets).

Example 3: Refugee

- A refugee is a person who is forced to leave his or her home country to escape from danger.
  - Imagine you only have ten minutes to leave your home. You can only take a rucksack with you. You cannot take any other item which is carried separately. You cannot ask anyone else to carry anything for you.
  - What will you take? Draw or write a list of the things which you will take inside a rucksack outline (see template in the online resources PDF). Which item would you keep if everything else had to be left behind?

Useful for

Enabling pupils to analyse what matters most to themselves and others (values clarification); encouraging empathy.

See also

Target board–94
Values auction–96
Diary of reflection–104
Online resources PDF

63 Moebius strip

Strategy

A Moebius strip is a twisted loop, normally made of paper, unusual for having only one side and one edge.

- Make a long strip of paper by cutting an A4 sheet into three lengthwise and joining the ends. Hold it as if to make a cylinder, then put in a half twist (180 degrees) and stick together.
- Ask pupils:
  - How many sides has it got? (Draw a line down the middle and find out.)
  - How many edges has it got? (Mark a point on the edge and run your fingernail around it.)
  - What do you expect to get if you cut along the line you drew down the middle of the paper?
  - How could you use this as a visual aid to talk about the way religion sees the world?

Useful for

Encouraging reflection on perceptions and how we 'see' life.

See also

Board games–67
Gift for life–69
Sentence completion–98

Useful for

Enabling pupils to reflect on what matters most to them (values clarification).

See also

Rucksack—64

Values auction—96

66 Personal statement

Strategy

- Put pupils into groups of five or six and identify a leader for each group. Each group member is given four cards and on each card writes down a statement on an issue relevant to their work in RE, e.g. an ethical issue such as animal testing, or meanings in life, or ideas about what happens when someone dies.

- The leader collects in the cards and shuffles them, deals out two cards to each member of the group and places the remainder on the table, face down. Moving clockwise round the group, each member in turn considers his or her cards and has an opportunity to exchange them.

- If players are satisfied with the statements on their cards, they can keep them. If not, one card may be exchanged at a time by selecting a new one from the pile on the table, and placing the rejected card at the bottom of the pile. The activity continues until everyone is satisfied with the cards they have.

- At the end, each pupil must explain and justify the cards kept.

Useful for

Helping pupils reflect on their goals in life and the realities of living.

See also

XY grid—57

Values auction—96

67 Board games

Strategy

- Talk with pupils about some of the board games they are familiar with. Ask them to identify the goal of the game, and what makes the game interesting (or not).

- Choose a game for pupils to play which is relevant to the unit of work they are studying. The following board games designed for RE are available from RE Today Services. Each gives full instructions for playing the game, as well as suggestions for follow-up work.

- Board games designed for RE from RE Today Services:
  - Values Game (about the importance of values) – *Opening up Respect* (Opening up Primary RE series), ed. Fiona Moss, ISBN 9781905893515.
  - Moksha Chitram Game (about dharma and karma) – *Opening up Hinduism* (Opening up Primary RE series), ed. Fiona Moss, ISBN 9781905893366.
  - Moksha Patuma (a game about chance, triumph and disaster) – *Questions: Beliefs and Teachings* (Questions in Secondary RE series), ed. Stephen Pett, ISBN 9781905893317.
  - Commitment Game (about clarifying commitments) – *Exploring Codes for Living* (Exploring a Theme Primary RE Series), ed. Joyce Mackley, ISBN 9781905893072.
  - The Evil Game (about evil) – *Evil & Goodness* (Developing Secondary RE series), ed. Joyce Mackley, ISBN 9781904024200.
  - Perfect Partners (about partnerships and marriage) – *Relationships* (Developing Secondary RE series), ed. Rosemary Rivett, ISBN 9781904024538.
  - Insight (about spirituality) - *Spiritual RE* (Engaging with Secondary RE series), ed. Lat Blaylock, ISBN 9781905893102.

68 Brainstorming

Strategy

Useful for

Establishing existing knowledge and understanding; generating ideas; sorting ideas.

- Select a key word or concept, such as justice, worship, peace, spiritual, love, service, freedom.

- Ask pupils to list as many ideas as they can that are related to the chosen word or concept. No comment should be made at this stage, the object being to get down as many ideas as possible in as short a time as possible. Allow two or three minutes for this.

- In pairs, groups or as a class, pupils then discuss their ideas, giving reasons for them. They sort and prioritise their ideas, identifying those that need further thought, research and discussion.

- Brainstorming is more effective in developing creative responses if pupils are allowed to challenge the ideas offered – not just accepting everything. Some form of ranking of the best or most fruitful ideas, encouraging comments on why some ideas are better than others, can help this process.

 See also

Paper and pen–60
Mind mapping–95

69 Gift for life

Strategy

Useful for

Identifying what is of value in life, for pupils themselves and for believers from different religious traditions.

- Give everyone two sheets of paper. Ask them to write down in the middle of one the word 'Gift'.
- Brainstorm everything that comes to mind. Ask the pupils to cross out any words which are things money can buy. Ask them to focus on 'gifts' which money cannot buy – spend one or two minutes in quiet reflection.

- Using the other sheet of paper, pupils write down, and illustrate if they want, something they would like to give the person on their left to 'help them on the journey of life'. Allow a few minutes and then ask everyone to pass on their gifts.

- Follow-up discussion – What gifts were received? What are pupils' thoughts about their gift?

- In small groups, follow the same process, imagining what a believer from a specific faith tradition might say. For example, a Christian might put Jesus, or love or justice; a Muslim might put the Holy Qur'an, ummah or prayer. Delete any that can be bought, then consider what gifts the group would offer the believer for the journey and why.

See also

Observation–58
Rucksack–64
Values auction–96

REFLECT

Useful for

Encouraging a sense of self-worth and the valuing of others; enabling pupils within a group to share personal experiences while encouraging others to be sensitive and appreciative towards the thoughts, feelings and values of others.

See also

Trust games–2
Affirmation–13
Values auction–96

70 Newsboards

Strategy

- Invite pupils to place on the newsboard items of personal interest or concern, e.g. a photograph of a family wedding; a certificate won playing a favourite sport; a [photograph of] an item given as a gift by someone loved by the pupil (e.g. an absent or deceased parent or relative).
- Provide opportunity to talk with pupils individually, and as a class, about the items shared on the newsboard, encouraging sensitivity and appreciation of what pupils have shared.

Useful for

Working with personally sensitive issues; establishing existing knowledge and understanding; generating ideas; sorting ideas.

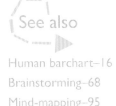

See also

Human barchart–16
Brainstorming–68
Mind-mapping–95

71 Paper and pen

Strategy

This strategy is a variation on brainstorming but is more suitable for personally sensitive issues which individuals may not wish to share publicly, e.g. 'My greatest fear'.

- Provide pupils with paper and pens and explain that they should not write their name on the paper: the task is to be anonymous.
- Ask pupils to write down the following headings: This lesson; School; Life in general. They should privately write down their greatest fear or worry concerning each. Each pupil then folds up their paper and places it into a container passed around by the teacher.
- The teacher reads out some of the responses, being careful not to identify anyone in the class. Commonly held worries and fears are identified for discussion.
- Put pupils in small groups and given them one fear or worry which is shared by many in the class. Groups suggest three things a person with that fear or worry could do.

Useful for

Expressing visions of life.

See also

Observation–58
Gift for life–69

72 Mobile phone

Strategy

- Following work on the role and significance of angels – for example, in the first revelation of the Qur'an (Islam) or the Christmas story (Christianity) – provide pupils with an illustration of a mobile phone, and ask them to create five messages to the human race from the angel of mercy, the angel of good news, the angel of death, the angel of hope and the fallen angel. What would the angels say to the human beings today?

TALK

Talking is an essential learning process. In RE, good teaching guides and structures the ways pupils talk about religion and belief, so that they learn a lot from each other. Talk also clarifies things for the person doing the talking. Children and young people often say that they especially value RE for the range of discussion and argument it provokes: teachers who want their lessons to be places of spiritual and moral development need good strategies to get pupils talking purposefully.

In this section you will find a wide variety of strategies that provide pupils with opportunities to express their ideas, understandings and questions in RE through talk: for example, through discussion, debate, buzz groups, dialogue using religious language accurately, questioning images, and careful observation.

There are pupil activity sheets to accompany some of the strategies; these are found in the online resources PDF which accompanies this publication.

Sources of stories, images and films are found on the inside back cover.

TALK

Useful for

Supporting younger pupils in identifying the main parts of a story.

See also

Freeze-frame–5
Re-enactment–7
Role play–9
Masks–24
What really matters?–50
Online resources PDF

73 Box story

Strategy

- Pupils, working individually or in groups, draw a picture from a faith story they are studying on each side of a cube. Each picture also has one or two words. The pictures can either be drawn on a template (see the online resources PDF) which is then made up into a cube, or pasted on to the sides of an existing box.
- Pupils throw the box from one to another. Each time it is caught the catcher must tell the part of the story that is uppermost. A variation could be to play music and only when it stops does the pupil holding the box tell the story.
- Stories might include: Queen Maya's Dream (Buddhism); Genesis Creation Story (Christianity); How Ganesha got his Elephant Head (Hinduism); Hanukkah (Judaism); The Birth of Guru Nanak (Sikhism).

Useful for

Enabling young pupils to look carefully at a picture to identify what it conveys; practising using accurate religious vocabulary.

See also

Drawing around–25
Picture extending–36
Pictures from memory–93

74 Rumour mill

Strategy

- Put pupils into groups of eight, and in each group identify pupils as Pair A, Pair B, Pair C and Pair D.
- Give Pair A in each group of eight a picture to look at for a short time, e.g. a baptism (Christianity); the outside of a mosque (Islam); a Torah scroll with mantle (Judaism). They describe the picture as fully as they can to Pair B. Pair B describes the picture to Pair C, who then describe it to Pair D. This generates confusion – it is a 'rumour mill' because the quality of description as it passes through the stages usually declines.
- Pair D draw what they have had described to them.
- Ask each group to reveal their drawing and compare what they did with the original. What were the key aspects of the picture that should have been described? What vocabulary should have been used?

Useful for

Encouraging paired or small-group discussion; consolidating learning.

See also

Reflection alley–53
Can of worms–76
Buzz groups–84
Talking circle–100

75 Yo-yo

Strategy

- Put pupils into pairs and identify them as A and B.
- Identify a topic for discussion. Person A starts off the discussion by making a brief statement, which Person B then 'picks up' and comments on or extends. Person A then responds to the comment or extension and Person B responds again, and so on, passing the statement back and forth, developing it as they go along.

76 Can of worms

Strategy

- Write a series of questions for discussion on a particular theme on slips of paper and put them in a jar or box. Questions can be devised by the pupils or teacher.
- Pass the jar round the group and ask pupils in turn to take a question and respond to it.
- Provide sentence starters for pupils to record their responses, for example:
  - I feel (angry) when …
  - My idea of heaven is …
  - My hope for the world is …
- When using this with a 'circle within a circle', pupils on the inside pick out a question each, the outer circle rotates, and the pupil asks the same question of each partner, noting down opinions for later feedback to the group as a whole. Outer and inner circles swap roles halfway through the activity.
- Alternatively, pupils could pull out a question and suggest how a Christian, Atheist, Muslim, for example, might answer.
- Or a series of questions for a visitor to the classroom to answer could be written, or a person acting in character in the hotseat.

Useful for

Exploring controversy; developing speaking and listening skills.

See also

Human barchart–16
Hotseat–17
Photoboard–30

77 Snowballing

Strategy

- Present pupils with a question, dilemma or issue for discussion.
- Ask each pupil to share his or her thoughts with a partner.
- Pairs then combine with another pair. They agree a group opinion or plan of action and either appoint a spokesperson to give a brief report back to the class, or use the plan of action to complete the task.

Example:

- Pupils studying religious teaching on rules for living can be given the 'rules for living' for one religion. They:
  - reflect on what they agree with or think is important, and anything they disagree with or don't understand
  - in pairs, exchange ideas and write down three 'codes for living' rules which they think matter most from the examples provided
  - in groups of four or six they compare and sort their ideas, identify 'rules for living' they wish to recommend to the class and appoint and brief a spokesperson
  - engage in whole class feedback from the groups
  - discuss key questions on the issue, e.g. Are there some principles that all groups agreed on? If we are agreed that these are good rules to live by, do we actually live by them?

Useful for

Encouraging the expression and justification of opinion.

See also

X Y grid–57
On the one hand … on the other hand–106

Useful for

Encouraging pupils to share understanding; developing speaking and listening skills.

See also

Feelings graph–97

Talking circle–100

Tenuous links–101

78 Talking sticks

Strategy

- Sit pupils in a circle and give one pupil a stick (or similar item).
- Read out a discussion starter and invite the person with the stick to comment. Only the person with the stick may speak. At first use 'non-threatening' topics for discussion, e.g. watching television. As the class gains confidence with the strategy, and with each other, topics can be more personal or controversial.
- Expect everyone to give the person speaking their full attention. When he or she has finished, the stick is passed to the next person, who comments on the original statement or a previous speaker's observations on it.
- Use a structure such as 'I agree/disagree with X because ….'

Useful for

Developing analytical reasoning and decision-making skills; values clarification; prioritising.

See also

Debate–81

Target board–94

Socratic questioning–115

79 Balloon debate

Strategy

- Ask pupils to imagine that they are crossing an ocean or desert in a hot-air balloon. In the balloon with them are seven or eight 'companions' – these can be values or people (see examples below). Halfway across, the balloon starts losing height rapidly and they are forced to make decisions about which of their companions should be thrown out in order for the balloon to stay in the air or, if they crash land, would give them the best chance of survival until they were rescued.
- Divide the class into small groups. One group forms a panel which will hear all the arguments and will make the decision about which value or person is saved and which is thrown overboard. The other groups each take one of the characters in the balloon and devise a strong argument for why their value or person should remain in the balloon, and others should be thrown out.
- Groups choose one of their members to be their spokesperson. Each spokesperson in turn presents the group's case to the panel. The panel then retire to make their decision, which they present to the full class, with reasons.
- Groups work together or as individuals to express their response to the decision with reasons.

Example:

- Put values in the balloon, such as love, hope, loyalty, faith, respect, equality, empathy, honesty, creativity, wisdom, commitment, forgiveness, humility, acceptance. Which of these are essential for survival, or building a harmonious community?

Example:

- Put people in the balloon, such as Archbishop Desmond Tutu (Anglican bishop and social rights activist); The Buddha (spiritual teacher and founder of Buddhism); Steve Jobs (entrepreneur and co-founder of Apple); Imran Khan (Pakistani Muslim politician and former international cricketer); Professor Robert Winston (Jewish medical doctor and scientist); Professor Brian Cox (physicist and TV presenter); a priest; an imam; a prime minister or national president. Which of these people's jobs or abilities make them more or less valuable to society?

80 Snowflake

Strategy

- Provide pupils with a simple line drawing of a snowflake by drawing four lines intersecting in the centre, creating eight spokes (see template in the online resources PDF).
- At the outer edge of each line or spoke, provide a statement for pupils to respond to (8 statements in all) e.g.
  - I believe that following a religion is the best way to live.
  - I believe that this life is a preparation for a new life after death.
  - I believe that I can help make the world a more peaceful place.
  - I believe that love is more important than freedom.
  - I believe that prayer is helpful.
  - I believe that God is real and not just in your imagination.
- Ask pupils, working individually, to put an X along the spoke to illustrate how far they agree with the statement at the end – the nearer the centre, the less they agree; the nearer the outside edge, the more they agree.
- Pupils then join up the Xs to make their unique snowflake shape. This forms the basis for discussion and debate with others as they compare each other's snowflakes.

With thanks to Sarah Northall, who developed this strategy while teaching at Chipping Norton School.

Useful for

Encouraging pupils to express their views with reasons and explanation.

See also

Talking sticks–78
Buttresses–114
Different audiences–116
Online resources PDF

81 Debate

Strategy

- Provide pupils with a carefully worded motion for a debate, or help them develop one of their own. For example:
  - This house believes that love of money is the root of all kinds of evil.
  - This house believes that prayer is answered.
  - This house believes that abortion is wrong in all circumstances.
- Two pupils, with supporters, prepare a speech to argue for the motion, and two pupils with supporters prepare a speech against the motion. The speech should last no more than five minutes. Provide pupils with adequate time and resources to prepare their speeches.
- Other pupils, also working in small groups, prepare short speeches to be made 'from the floor' to lend support to one side. These speeches should last no more than two minutes. Again, time and resources will need to be provided.
- Hold the debate. The four main speakers address the floor first, followed by speeches and questions 'from the floor'.
- At the end of the debate a vote is taken and the motion is either 'carried' or 'defeated'.
- Pupils, individually or in small groups, prepare a response to the outcome of the debate, reflecting their own considered opinion on the motion. They include a suggestion of how members of a particular religion might respond to the motion.

Useful for

Developing skills of employing argument and anticipating and evaluating the arguments of others.

See also

Balloon debate–79
On the one hand . . . on the other hand–106
Socratic questioning–115

TALK

82 Agenda-setting

Strategy

- Devise an agenda of questions for small discussion groups, taking care to challenge pupils to address all the key aspects of the topic. These can also be used to guide research and enquiry outside the classroom.
- Provide news articles describing six real-life conflict situations. Read these out (or ask pupils to) and ask pupils to visualise what it is like for the real people in these situations.

Example: exploring conflict

- Divide pupils into six groups, each group taking one of the conflict scenarios. They analyse the problem using the following questions:

  - What is the problem?
  - Who is affected?
  - Where does it happen?
  - Why does it happen?
  - How could it be tackled?
  - What is the best way forward?
  - Who will take action?

- Follow-up discussion could focus on:
  - Which of the questions above is the most difficult to answer? Why?
  - Are there any causes of conflict that are common to all the situations?
  - Have you experienced any of these causes of conflict in your own life?
  - Who should take action? Why?

83 Mystery bag

Strategy

- Put an artefact in a cloth bag which has a large question mark on it and a drawstring. Artefacts might include: a Buddha image (Buddhism); a chalice (Christianity); tasbih or prayer beads (Islam); a shofar (Judaism); a diva or arti lamp (Hinduism); a karah (Sikhism).
- Pass the bag round the group. Ask pupils to feel the object carefully through the bag and suggest adjectives to describe it. After reflection, ask them to guess what it is and suggest how it might be used. Alternatively ask a pupil to describe the object, and others to listen and sketch it.

84 Buzz groups

Strategy

- Give pupils two minutes to talk to one or two others about a specific topic or their reaction to something they have just seen or heard. Move to new groups and report a comment they made and one other comment they heard. Keep the activity short and snappy to catch first reactions without getting involved in a full discussion.
- Examples: immediate response to a speaker, a presentation or video clip.

85 Just a minute

Strategy

- Identify a topic and ask a pupil to speak on that topic for one minute without hesitation, deviation or repetition. S/he may be challenged by any pupil on the grounds of breaking one of those rules.
- Award points to the challenger for a correct challenge. The challenger then takes over the speaking for the remaining time, unless successfully challenged.
- Points are awarded to the speaker for an incorrect challenge and for being the one who is speaking when the 60 seconds are up. An extra point is given to a speaker who completes the 60 seconds without being successfully interrupted.
- Topics might include: things to be thankful for; the importance of Christmas; saying sorry; what matters most in life; life after death; good and evil.

Useful for

Consolidating learning; focusing attention on key points and issues.

See also

News bulletins–6
Post-it®s–54
Wall of wisdom–56

86 Rainbow groups

Strategy

- After small group activity, each member of the group is given a number (e.g. 1–5) or colour. All pupils with the same number or colour re-form into new groups.
- In the new groups, pupils take it in turns to report back on the findings and achievements of their previous group.

Example:

- Pupils explore religious beliefs about marriage in groups with a focus on one religion. On completion the groups are reorganised. The task of the new group is to identify similarities and differences in the beliefs and teaching of the different religions studied.

Useful for

Supporting informed and evaluative essay writing.

See also

Envoys–42
On the one hand … on the other hand–106
Buttresses–114

87 Questioning images

Strategy

- Lay out a selection of images on large sheets of paper (one picture per piece of paper). They should show aspects of contemporary religious belief and practice in one or two religions, e.g. a church wedding, a baby being baptised and a Nativity set (Christianity); a boy reading the Qur'an, Friday prayers in a mosque, and giving zakat (Islam).
- Ask pupils to walk around and think of questions to ask about the pictures, and then write their questions on the paper around the relevant image.
- With younger pupils, you might pair them up – a writer with a non-writer; or you might have a TA or parent acting as scribe for a group of children.
- Collect together the question sheets and use them as the basis for discussion about the pictures.

Useful for

Encouraging observation and enquiry skills in younger pupils.

See also

In the gallery–22
Photoboard–30
Pictures from memory–93

Useful for

Developing observation and speculation skills in younger pupils.

See also

Paintbox–19

Bubbling speech . . . bubbling thoughts–52

Mysteries–49

88 Through the keyhole

Strategy

- Choose an image or a video clip and cover up most of the image, leaving just a small section visible. This can be done using a 'reveal' or 'spotlight' tool on many IWBs, or paste the image into word-processing software and cover up parts with boxes.
- If using a video clip, try and choose one with sounds: for example, a Hindu priest waking the deities in the temple, ringing a bell as part of the ritual (see: www.cleo.net.uk).
- Ask pupils to say what they can see. Move the 'spotlight' around the image, showing different parts of the whole. Again, ask what they can see.
- Gradually reveal more of the image, allowing pupils to describe more and try to guess what the whole image is. Encourage them to ask questions about what might be 'through the keyhole'. Finally reveal the whole image and ask pupils to suggest how they went about identifying what it might be.
- A variation is to:
  - Show pupils a collection of items which might be found in the home of a person of a particular religion and ask them to suggest which religion and what it tells them about the person who would have such items in their home.
  - For example: A Hindu family home might contain: murtis or images of gods and goddesses; an arti tray; a copy of the Bhagavad Gita; divas (lamps used to celebrate Divali); rachis (wristbands given by siblings at Raksha Bandhan).

Useful for

Stimulating discussion and decision-making.

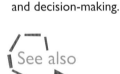

See also

Role play–9

Yes or no–55

X Y grid–57

Values auction–96

89 Yardstick

Strategy

- Give pupils a statement to serve as a 'yardstick', a standard to measure everything else by, such as 'Treat others as you would like to be treated yourself.'
- Give pupils, or ask them to devise for themselves, dilemmas or situations in which the yardstick has to be applied.

Example

- Yardstick: You should always tell your teacher if someone does something wrong.
- Dilemma: What would you do if the pupil who has done something wrong is:
  - someone you don't like?
  - your best friend?
  - you?

Example

- Yardstick: It is always wrong to take life.
- Dilemma: What would you do if you were:
  - in the army and being sent to fight in a war?
  - a doctor deciding whether or not to allow a rape victim to have an abortion?
  - a man or woman whose wife or husband is being threatened by an armed robber?

THINK

What some teachers call 'thinking skills', others say are 'just good learning'. Either way, pupils are better at RE if they can compare different examples, identify and explain similarities and differences, rank, sort and order examples. Their RE tasks need to include making balanced judgements, noticing implications and possibilities, speculating or arguing effectively. These skills in RE and in education generally are developed through practice, so the classroom should be a thinking place.

In this section you will find a wide variety of strategies that provide pupils with opportunities to develop their ideas, understandings and questions in RE in a reflective and thoughtful way, for example through careful observation, discerning the meaning of text, research, clarifying ideas, valuing the opinions of others, engaging in discussion and questioning, and deep thinking about concepts and issues.

There are pupil activity sheets to accompany some of the strategies: these are found in the online resources PDF.

Sources of stories, images and films are found on the inside back cover.

MIND MAPPING

TARGET BOARD

SIMILARITIES AND DIFFERENCES

PICTURES FROM MEMORY

JIGSAW READINGS

TALKING CIRCLE

Useful for

Clarifying the meaning of ideas; using existing knowledge as a bridge to new understanding; establishing prior understanding.

See also

Puzzling questions–38
Mysteries–29
Disentangling–107
Online resources PDF

90 Similarities and differences (Odd one out)

Strategy

- Put pupils into pairs or small groups and give them a set of three concepts, pictures or ideas.
- Ask pupils to analyse the characteristics of each concept, picture or idea: What is unique to each? What is shared by each pair? What is shared by all?
- Provide a framework for pupils to record their thinking in. A simple Venn diagram is one structure. There are two detailed templates in the online resources PDF.

Examples

- Muslim family at prayer – Muslim boy reading the Qur'an – aqiqah ceremony
- Church – gurdwara – mosque
- Muslim – Christian – Jew
- Brahma – Shiva – Vishnu
- Roman Catholic – Baptist – Quaker
- Embryo – foetus – baby
- Design – accident – evolution
- Knowing – believing – holding an opinion

Useful for

Identifying different types of questions.

See also

Puzzling questions–38
Good questions, better questions–44
Online resources PDF

91 Zebra

Strategy

- Provide each group of pupils with a 'board' which is a piece of paper coloured black on the right-hand third, white on the left-hand third and grey in the centre. There is a template in the online resources PDF.
- Sit pupils in groups of three or four around the board. Give them a pile of 10–15 cards with statements on them which require the answers yes or no, true or false, e.g. Guru Nanak is the first Sikh Guru; All Sikhs wear turbans; Sikhs are vegetarian.
- Each pupil takes it in turn to pick up a card and place it on the board; they place correct statements on the black section and incorrect statements on the white section of the board, giving reasons.
- Players may move any card they think has been wrongly placed, when it comes to their turn, but they must justify their decision.
- On completion, and when all have agreed the placings, pupils are given a second set of 10 –15 cards. The activity is repeated but these statements need more subtle answers or require value judgements, e.g. 'Going to the gurdwara is important'.
- Pupils realise that there are no clear-cut answers to the questions – and the grey area comes into play. This can be used with a number of statements about belief, e.g. about God or life after death.
- Variation: Mix the two types of card up and ask them to place them on the black and white sections of the board. How long does it take them to realise there are two different types of questions? What solutions do they offer?

Odd one out: Islam

I can see . . .

Similarities between 1 and 2

Differences between 1 and 2

I can see . . .

The odd one out is . . .

because . . .

Similarities between 1 and 3

Similarities between 2 and 3

Differences between 1 and 3

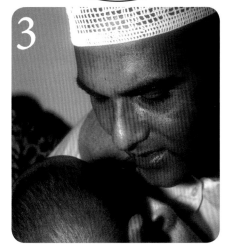

Differences between 2 and 3

I can see . . .

Useful for

Clarifying differences between different types of questions.

See also

92 Ultimate questions

Strategy

- Prepare strips of coloured paper representing colours of the rainbow. Each colour represents a different aspect of human experience: for example, Life (red), Death (orange), Humanity (yellow), The earth (green), Good (blue,; Evil (indigo), God (violet).

- Pupils think of as many questions as possible that no one can answer, under each of these headings, and write them on the appropriate coloured strip. Mix up all the strips in a container so that questions are not attributable to individuals, and then sort them into their colours.

- Put pupils into seven groups, one for each colour. Ask pupils to sift the questions (some of which will be very similar), and reduce them to a manageable number for display while ensuring that these include the questions the pupils think are most important. These are then used to create a 'rainbow' of ultimate questions.

- In groups of four, pupils identify four questions from the 'rainbow' they would want to ask God to answer if they could. Taking responsibility for one question each (but working in pairs), they research what 'answers' members of different faiths might suggest and could give.

- Working individually, pupils then choose one question and prepare a short presentation explaining why they think it interesting and important, gathering a range of responses to the question. It's good to ask for at least three different answers, encouraging divergent thinking.

Useful for

Encouraging careful observation and teamwork; interpreting and analysing images.

See also

93 Pictures from memory

Strategy

- Choose a picture that is relevant to the topic being studied and which will contribute to pupils' understanding of the current topic. The internet is a good source of images that can be downloaded and printed for class use. Pictures might include a mandala (Buddhism); the Crucifixion (Christianity); pilgrims on Hajj to Makkah (Islam); reading the Guru Granth Sahib (Sikhism). A short film showing this strategy in action is found on www.natre.org.uk.

- Organise the class into groups of four or five and explain to them that they are to produce a group representation of a picture using a series of 10-second exposures to it.

- Invite one pupil from each group (Person A) to come to the front of the room to look at the picture for 10 seconds. Person A then returns to the group and describes the picture so that Person B can draw it. Person B then goes to the front to look at the picture, and returns to describe what s/he saw so that Person C can add to the drawing, and so on. Other group members ask questions of the describer that can only be answered with 'Yes' or 'No'. They also plan their strategy for the next person to view the picture, for example what part of the picture to focus on.

- Repeat the activity until each group member has viewed the picture and reported back. Keep the picture covered between viewings, and don't allow anyone to bring paper and pencil to their viewing.

- Reveal the picture. Ask pupils to decide which group did the most accurate copy or had the correct details, and so on.

- Follow up the activity with discussion about what they found in the picture, how it connects to their prior learning and identify questions for ongoing research and discussion. Ask pupils about the strategies they used, and how they might approach the task next time.

94 Target board

Strategy

- Draw five concentric circles, like a bull's-eye on a dartboard, on a large piece of paper (There is a template in the online resources PDF). The central circle represents 'Essential', the second 'Very important', the third 'Important', the fourth 'Quite good' and the fifth 'Not such a good idea'. This provides a structure to help pupils evaluate, sort and rank statements.
- Provide pupils with a series of statements drawn from a story, or relating to religious beliefs, values and practices, or a moral issue such as abortion or war.
- In pairs or small groups, pupils discuss each statement and place it on the board, justifying their decision as they do so. Only one card can be placed at the centre (Essential). Once placed, cards can only be moved by agreement of the group.

Example: A better world

- Provide pupils with a copy of the target board and 12 statements from world religions that capture their vision of what the world would be like if people were more God-centred and less self-centred (see below). Provide some blank cards for pupils to add their own ideas.
- When all the cards are on the board, pupils should:
  - work out some arguments to justify identifying some ideas as 'essential' and some as 'not such a good idea'
  - identify what it would take to live up to these ideas
  - feed back their thoughts to the class.

Example: What matters most?

- Provide a selection of concepts and practices from a religion, and ask pupils to suggest which matters most to believers, e.g. Hajj, Holy Qur'an, declaration of faith, Friday prayers.

Useful for

Developing skills of analysis and evaluation; values clarification; developing speaking and listening skills.

See also

Interviewing—43
What really matters—50
Online resources PDF

All life is sacred.	Everyone should be valued as an individual.	Serve others, asking for nothing in return.
Adopt a non-violent approach to life, respecting all living creatures.	Everyone has a responsibility for others.	There is no greater love than laying down your life for your friends.
It is better to give than to receive.	Forgive as you would like to be forgiven.	Treat others as you would like to be treated yourself.
Live truthfully.	Talking can bring peace because it brings greater understanding.	Treat others with justice and kindness.

 Photocopy permission

Useful for

Clarifying thinking; processing information; organising ideas; making connections between areas of learning; developing critical thinking skills; analysing information.

See also

Human barchart–16

X Y grid–57

Socratic questioning–115

95 Mind-mapping

Strategy

- A mind map is a way of visually presenting an idea or theme by writing down words and making links between the ideas as branches. It may look like a tree or river with many branches and sub-branches.
- Mind maps can be created with paper and marker pens, or by using mind mapping software. They are most effective when different colours are used to represent different qualities of relationship, or sub-categories of those qualities.
- Identify a key theme or idea which is relevant to pupils' learning and ask them to:
  - draw a symbol for it in the centre of an A4 piece of paper (landscape)
  - draw a big line coming out from this symbol for each of the main ideas associated with the topic. Add a picture at the end of each line to represent the idea.
  - draw smaller lines coming off each big line, one for each relevant thought, question or example.

Useful for

Prioritising personal values; developing decision-making skills; encouraging whole-class involvement.

See also

Rucksack–64

Personal statement–66

Board games–67

Gift for life–69

96 Values auction

Strategy

- Get pupils to create and photocopy a list of different types of values. Some examples are given below, but adapt this list to make it appropriate to the topic under discussion and to keep it up to date.
- Make coloured cards to represent different amounts of money. Each group will need £1,000 in mixed cards (e.g. 12 x £50; 12 x £20; 8 x £10; 12 x £5; 20 x £1).
- Put the class into groups of up to four, and give each group a list of the values and £1,000 in mixed cards.
- Give the groups 10 minutes to look through the list of values and decide which are worth most to their lives. When the auction starts they will be asked to bid for the things they value. The highest bidder will receive the item.
- Auction off each item in turn until everything is sold.
- Follow-up discussion
  - Which items received the most bids, and why?
  - Which items received few bids, and why?
  - What other things do people in the group value that were not on the list?
  - What reasons do people give for their bids? Why do they believe that these are important?
  - What kinds of things influence our values? (Consider: faith, upbringing, peer pressure, etc).
  - Who or what decides our values?
- Values
  - Popularity; good parent/carer; good health; friends; freedom; good education; self-discipline; having fun; sporting skills; feeling safe; honesty; vegetarianism; celebrity; religious faith; clean environment; love; family; space to be alone; a pet; enough to eat; a big house; a special talent; intelligence; designer clothes; sight.

97 Feelings graph

Strategy

- Choose a story in which the fortunes or feelings of one of the characters changes over the course of the story. Prepare a series of 8–12 cards, each containing a statement about the story. Make enough sets of cards for each small group of pupils. The materials for Muhammad's Night of Power (Islam) are provided below and in the online resources PDF. Suggestions of other stories are provided on page 79.

- Provide a simple template for a graph (i.e. an x and a y axis). Space the words 'Beginning', 'Middle' and 'End' along the horizontal axis. Put three images or words which represent a spectrum of emotion (e.g. 'Very happy', 'OK', 'Miserable') along the vertical axis. Pupils can decide these words or the teacher can provide them. See the online resources PDF for templates.

- Read the story with the pupils, asking them to focus in particular on one of the characters. In small groups, ask each group to:
  - read and think about the series of statements on the cards
  - decide together where on the graph the chosen character's emotions could be and why
  - report back to the whole class on decisions made
  - reflect on their thinking – for example, how did they arrive at the conclusions they did?

Examples:

- The Life of Siddhartha Gautama (Buddhism)
- Holy Week (Christianity)
- The Exile and Return of Lord Rama and Princess Sita (Hinduism)
- The Night of Power (Islam)
- The Passover (Judaism)
- The story of Baisakhi and Guru Gobind Singh (Sikhism)

Variations:

- Put two or more characters on the same graph, noting similarities and differences.
- Ask pupils to provide the statements for a given feelings graph.
- Ask pupils to select six statements which they consider to be most significant from a piece of text, and place them on the feelings graph, explaining their rationale.

Useful for
Engaging deeply with a piece of text; interpreting information; exploring and justifying opinion; encouraging empathy.

See also

Guided story–63
Bag of words–109
Perspectival reading–112
Online resources PDF

Muhammad returns to Makkah from a long trip. He is hot and very tired.	Muhammad goes to a cave at Hira to pray to God and enjoy the peacefulness.	Suddenly Muhammad feels he is not alone. The angel Jibril is beside him.
Jibril insists that Muhammad reads from a scroll, even when he protests that he cannot read.	Eventually Muhammad reads the words! He repeats them to help him remember them.	Muhammad goes home and tells Khadijah, his wife, all that has happened.
Muhammad wonders what he will do if Khadijah doesn't believe him.	Eventually Khadijah says that she believes that the words are from Allah (God).	Muhammad tells many other people what happened. Not everyone believes him.

👁 Photocopy permission

THINK

The Night of Power

The Qur'an is revealed to Muhammad

The city of Makkah was hot and sticky, and crowded with many visitors. Muhammad had just returned from a long trip, and wanted to get away from the busy and noisy city to somewhere quiet and peaceful where he could be alone to talk to God.

He told his wife, Khadijah, that he was going to the cave called Hira in the nearby mountains. It was a cave he often went to when he wanted to think and pray.

The cave was quiet and cool. At last he had some time to pray and to be alone to think.

Suddenly he had a strange feeling. He felt as though he wasn't alone, that someone else was there! He slowly turned around, and in the corner near the entrance to the cave he could see a light. He looked more closely, squinting his eyes to get a better view. Then he realised it wasn't a light at all – it was an angel!

The angel, who was called Jibril, held out a scroll of paper which had words written on it. 'Read this, Muhammad,' the angel said. 'But I can't read,' replied Muhammad. Once again the angel told him to read the words on the scroll, and, once again, Muhammad told the angel that he could not read. A third time the angel told him to read the scroll, in the name of the Lord who created the world.

This time Muhammad found that he could read the words on the scroll, and as he read them he felt as though the words were being written on his heart. Muhammad repeated the words, and then he knew that he would never forget them.

Muhammad left the cave and returned to the city of Makkah to tell his wife, Khadijah, all about what had happened to him in the cave. She knew immediately just how important these words were. She realised the words were from God.

In the following months and years Muhammad received many more words from God, and he told them to many people who also believed they were from God. Some people in Makkah believed what he said was true, and others did not like what he was saying.

Years later, Muhammad died. Then the people who believed what Muhammad had said to be true wrote down all the words that Muhammad had been told by the angel Jibril, so that the words would never be forgotten. The book they were written in is called the Qur'an. The word Qur'an means 'that which is read or recited'.

Photocopy permission

98 Sentence completion

Strategy

- Write an unfinished sentence on the board as a means of stimulating thought and reflection. Ask pupils to complete the sentence either orally or in writing, then share their ideas with the class. Some or all responses could be recorded on the board for all to see, and as a stimulus to further discussion.
- Sentence starters can be used in a variety of contexts, for example:
  - Starting discussion
    - My idea of heaven is …
    - My hope for the world is …
  - Expressing feelings
    - I feel happy when …
  - Observation
    - I noticed …
  - Negotiation
    - I would like to …

Useful for

Reflective thinking; clarification of thoughts, feelings and opinions; promoting listening skills

See also

Wall of wisdom–56
Can of worms–76
Talking sticks–78

99 Jigsaw reading

Strategy

With younger pupils

- Choose a series of pictures which tell a story. Provide sets of these pictures for each small group of pupils. See the Easter Story example in the online resources PDF.
- Ask pupils to talk in their groups about what they can see in each of the pictures and then put the pictures in the correct order so that they tell the story.
- The final version can be stuck on a large sheet of paper and used as a basis for ongoing work, e.g. recording further questions for follow up and discussion.

With older pupils

- Choose a coherent and well-structured piece of text, a story or a narrative account of a moral dilemma (see conjoined twins example on the next page and in the online resources PDF). Cut the text up into a number of pieces, jumble them up and give a set to each group of three or four pupils.
- Ask pupils to read out each section in their group and piece the text back together in a coherent order (which may not be quite the same as the original).
- The final version can be stuck on a large sheet of paper and used as a basis for ongoing work, e.g. recording further questions for follow up and discussion.

Examples:

- Faith stories: e.g. The Night of Power – the Qur'an is Revealed to Muhammad (Islam); The Walk to Emmaus (Christianity); The Founding of the Khalsa (Sikhism).
- The Four Noble Truths (Buddhism)
- The Apostles' Creed (Christianity)

Useful for

Discerning the meaning of text; encouraging co-operative working.

See also

Disentangling–107
Form criticism–111
Silent conversations–113
Online resources PDF

Jigsaw reading: Conjoined twins

Should doctors or parents decide if one conjoined twin should die so that the other can live?

Task

- In groups of four, sort the 18 statements your teacher will give you to reconstruct the story of this religious and moral dilemma, establish lines of argument and work out who you think said what and why.
- After sorting the story line, allocate one of the following roles to each of the four members of the group:
  - The priest (the Roman Catholic Christian position)
  - The judge (the legal position)
  - The professor of ethics (ethical position)
  - The commentator (the observer's point of view).
- Regroup into specialist groups (i.e. all the 'priests' together) to do further research to help each other prepare for a role-play discussion.
- Return to your home groups. Role-play the discussion between the priest, the judge and the professor, with the commentator acting as observer and recorder. Each group feeds back, through the observer, the main issues and points raised.

Statements for sorting

The court should have allowed the parents to decide.	If there is no operation, it is likely both children will die.	Either decision is a tragic decision. If they decide to leave God's will to happen, then both children will die.
We leave it in the hands of God. We have no right, no power about life. Life is in the hands of God.	When we start, as humans, deciding who lives and who dies … I feel very uncomfortable.	The question is simple – do you kill one to save the other, or do you let two die?
If they decide to intervene or let the doctors intervene, then they will in effect be responsible for the death of one of the children in order to save the other.	For their parents, the operation is not a question of life or death. It is a test of their faith.	Two baby girls joined at the lower abdomen lie entwined in a hospital incubator in Manchester. One must die so the other can live.
As Roman Catholics they believe that it is wrong to do evil – sanctioning the death of a child – even though it could result in good.	These parents do not have weird views. They have very standard views, the most important of which is you don't kill one person in order to save another.	I think it's wrong. I think this is a classic example of a moral dilemma where two standard positions are in a clashing situation.
The pain of being on the sharp horns of this dilemma is excruciating because you do worry – and you do your best.	If there is hope that one of them can survive, they can separate and let one live.	Whose job is it to decide questions of life or death? The court's. Not a job we have to do, most certainly.

Photocopy permission

100 Talking circle (speed dating)

Strategy

Useful for

Encouraging deep thinking about a concept or issue.

See also

Question box–39
Balloon debate–79
Socratic questioning–115

- Arrange the classroom in an inner and outer circle of chairs so that all pupils can sit facing one other person. This is sometimes called 'speed dating' because of the layout of the chairs, not the topic of conversation!
- Provide 15 quotations or statements about the chosen concept or issue and give each pupil in the outer circle one of the 15 quotations. Quotations to support work on Forgiveness, and a response sheet, are provided in the online resources PDF.
- Pupils with the quotation card read aloud the statement to the pupil opposite. They each say what they think it means and whether they agree with it, and then write their thoughts in a sentence on a recording sheet.
- Every two minutes the teacher signals for everyone in the outside circle to move on one seat. This means that everyone gets a new partner, and a new quotation to discuss.
- Provide follow-up work, e.g. asking pupils to record their personal responses to the following sentence prompts. For work on forgiveness the prompts might include:
  - I think saying sorry is important when …
  - Forgiveness can be very difficult, for example …
  - Forgiveness can be the best thing to do because …
  - If someone asked for my advice about forgiving a person who harmed them, I'd say …
  - Another thing I thought about from this work was …

101 Tenous links

Strategy

Useful for

Clarifying thinking; supporting ability to analyse and synthesise.

See also

Analysing questions–45
Secret agent–105
Turn one thing into another–110

- Like the radio game of how to get from one song to another, give pupils a list of key concepts and ideas in a topic they are studying. Include: key writers, scholars, faith representatives, texts, stories, and so on.
- Select two and ask pupils to get from one to another, in as many steps as they like.

102 Fact or opinion

Strategy

Useful for

Distinguishing fact from fiction; clarifying thinking.

See also

Mysteries–49
Yes or no–55
Different audiences–116

- Arrange pupils into pairs, and give each pair a set of statements about a topic they are studying. The statements should contain a mix of fact and opinion. Examples for 'Prayer in Islam' and 'Religion and Science' are found on the next page and in the online resources PDF.
- Ask pupils to read each card to their partners and decide together whether it is expressing a fact or an opinion. They should discuss any statement about which they are unsure, or which they find difficult to classify as 'fact' or 'opinion'.

THINK

Fact or opinion? Prayer in Islam

When I pray I am worshipping God and I am talking to Allah.	Muslims pray five times a day.	I know that if I have prayed with all my concentration and my heart and for the sake of Allah, then I will be rewarded.
Du'a is a personal prayer. It often contains requests to God.	Prayer makes me think that God is there for me and will forgive me if I should do something wrong.	During Ramadan there is one extra prayer time each day.
Prayer makes me feel more alive and responsible. It makes me feel strength in my faith, and develops a generous community.	God answers prayer.	Some people are lazy and miss their prayers.

Fact or opinion? Religion and science

Some religious people believe that a universe without the idea of God is inexplicable.	The book of Genesis in the Bible describes literally how God created the universe.	Nicholas Copernicus discovered that the sun is at the centre of the universe.
Science will never find evidence of a link between apes and human beings.	Some scientists believe in a creator God as well as the Big Bang and evolution. Evolution is the mechanism through which God's creation took place.	Science will, eventually, discover all the laws of the universe.
The study of genetics explains how natural selection occurs.	God is no longer needed as an explanation.	The universe is about 15 billion years old.

Photocopy permission

WRITE

Many teachers note that pupils show good skills in discussion, but do not capture their best ideas in writing. This is often because writing tasks are not sharp enough, or not imaginative enough. So RE learning needs excellent task setting, so that writing is purposeful, clearly develops ideas and concepts, and promotes reflection and thinking. Younger children can write well in RE when the stimulus is interesting and the words are accessible. Imaginative and creative storytelling, for example, is a good starting point.

In this section you will find a wide variety of strategies that provide pupils with opportunities to develop their ideas, understandings and questions in RE through study of the writings of others and written responses of their own, for example through diaries of reflection, Socratic questioning, distinguishing between a variety of beliefs and interpretations, perspectival reading, form criticism, evaluative essay writing, and critical thinking about texts, stories and images.

There are pupil activity sheets to accompany some of the strategies; these are found in the online resources PDF.

Sources of stories, images and films are found on the inside back cover.

Useful for

Developing understanding and persuasive writing skills.

See also

Agony aunts–108
Different audiences–116

103 Write the blurb

Strategy

- Choose a short film clip (e.g. five minutes) which is relevant to the topic pupils are studying and give pupils the opportunity to watch it a couple of times. As they watch, ask pupils to identify key words and messages.
- Ask pupils to imagine that the film is going to be produced as a DVD for distribution, and their job is to write a 50–100 word blurb for the cover. This needs to say what the clip is about and why it is worth watching.

Useful for

Providing pupils with opportunities for quiet, structured reflection on issues of spiritual and moral worth or concern.

See also

Wall of wisdom–56
Observation–58
Rucksack–64
Personal statement–66

104 Diary of reflection

Strategy

- Build into lesson activities, on a regular basis, opportunities for pupils to express their ideas and insights into the work they have completed in the form of a confidential diary entry. Sentence starters for entries can be provided by the teacher.
- Basic ground rules:
  - Diaries of reflection are most effective when pupils are given regular opportunities to complete them as a quiet, disciplined exercise in an atmosphere of reflection.
  - Sentence starters can be written on the board and used as a starting point. As pupils get more experienced with this activity, encourage them to suggest the starting points … but always have some suggestions of your own ready.
  - Confidentiality must be respected. No pupil's reflections must be read out or seen by other pupils, or teachers other than the class teacher, without the pupils' permission.
  - Pupils should know that their diaries are valued and stored securely by the teacher.
  - From time to time the teacher should write a positive, encouraging or questioning comment in response to one of the pupils' reflections. These might be on sticky notes, in order to maintain the privacy of the book for pupils.

Useful for

Developing investigative writing skills.

See also

Fact or opinion–102
Different audiences–116

105 Secret agent

Strategy

- Pupils are secret agents. Their task is to infiltrate a particular group of people and report back to their employer on the actions/beliefs/behaviour of the group. The purpose of the investigation is to establish whether the group qualifies for an award, e.g. the 'Award for Equality'.
- Provide pupils with the resources to carry out their investigation (e.g. books, internet access, videos) and a simple structure for their report, asking for their evaluation of whether or not the group qualifies for the Award, with their reasons clearly explained.

106 On one hand... on the other hand

Useful for
Developing evaluative essay-writing skills.

See also

Mysteries—49
Agenda-setting—82
Debate—81

Strategy

- Provide students with stimulus material that presents someone's perspective on an issue or belief relevant to their studies, for example the perspective of an atheist or religious believer.

- Give pupils time to read the stimulus and then ask them to 'traffic light' the text: for example, marking in green the bits that make sense, in orange the bits they are unsure about, and in red the bits they don't understand.

- Pupils then pair up with someone else to see if they can help each other with the orange and red sections. They then work together to summarise the main points of the text they are studying in 30 words. These summaries can be shared with the class to see who has got the clearest account of the perspective being studied.

- Individually, pupils write a few sentences to say whether they agree or disagree with the perspective they are considering. These can be shared with the class so that a range of responses and the reasons for them are aired.

- Pupils then write an evaluative response to the stimulus materials; using the following sentence starters as a structure. They do not need to use all the sentence- starters but they must use the first one in each section.

First response

- **It is clear from [Name]'s statement that s/he thinks ...**
- S/he backs up her/his ideas by ...
- In addition ...
- We can see, therefore, that ...
- If [Name] is right, this means that ...
- Taking this idea further ...
- This view is ...
- [Name] is not saying that ...

Opposing point of view

- **On the other hand, some people disagree because ...**
- One example that supports this view is ...
- Another example is ...
- These examples show that ...
- This would mean that ...
- However, you might still say ...
- I would expect religious believers to say ...
- In contrast ...

Conclusion

- **I think that ... because ...**
- My first response to this question was ... because ...
- I changed/did not change my mind because ...
- The most persuasive evidence was ... because ...
- I agree with ...
- I disagree with ...
- I think that both views are ...

Useful for

Distinguishing between a variety of beliefs and interpretations.

See also

Mysteries–49

Fact or opinion–102

Perspectival reading–112

Online resources PDF

107 Disentangling

Strategy

- Provide pupils with composite or tangled-up versions of two pieces of text: for example, the same text in two different translations or text from two different religions on the same topic or theme. Two examples are given below; materials for the classroom are provided in the online resources PDF.

- Ask pupils to read the text carefully and then use different coloured pens to underline or highlight each translation (or the beliefs of each religion) in a different colour.

- Pupils then read the correct versions. They talk about what they have noticed, respond to questions about the texts to clarify understanding, analyse content and suggest areas for further enquiry.

Example 1 (younger pupils)

Disentangling translations: Parable of the Lost Son, Bible, Luke 15: 11-32 (Christianity) –see the online resources PDF.

- Translations: Wycliffe Bible c1400; Eugene Petersen, *The Message*, 2002. See wwwbiblegateway.com
- Activity: Pupils talk about their responses to the following questions:
  - What are the differences between the translations?
  - Which translation is easier to read and why?
  - Why do Christians make new translations?
  - Can you think of any potential problems with using translations of such ancient texts? For example, what happens when you don't know what a word means, such as grutched, nighed or wroth?

Example 2 (older pupils)

Disentangling beliefs: Life after death (Buddhism and Christianity)

- Sources: Buddhist Dhammapada 147–151; Christian Bible, 2 Corinthians 4: 16 – 5:10 – see online resources PDF.
- Activity:
  - Using a Venn diagram, pupils make notes on the differences between the Buddhist and Christian beliefs expressed. They should note in the overlap any similarities between the beliefs.
  - Pupils construct their own version of this for a different topic, such as Christian and Muslim teachings on justice, or the sanctity of life, and get their classmates to disentangle the texts.

Useful for

Applying religious and moral teaching a given situation.

See also

Enquiring into religious practice–48

Reflection alley–53

Jigsaw reading–99

108 Agony aunts

Strategy

- Present pupils with a letter to an agony aunt about an issue they have been studying. Pupils write the response, drawing on their learning in RE.

Examples:

- Dear Agony Aunt, My best friend recently broke off our friendship. Sam started saying all kinds of nasty things about me to some new friends. It really hurt. Sam has now come back and said sorry. I don't know what to do. It's hard to forgive.

- Dear Agony Aunt, I am a practising Hindu and have met a really nice boy at school. He's asked me to go out with him. He's not a Hindu and I don't think my parents will let me go. I'm 15. What should I do?

109 Bag of words

Strategy

- Choose a poem which presents some provocative and challenging thoughts relevant to the topic pupils are studying in RE. The poem 'Shopping with the Buddha' by Srivati is provided as an example in the online resources PDF.
- As pupils enter the classroom, give them a phrase or sentence from the poem and ask them to find a partner whose phrase is linked in some way. Don't tell pupils the title of the poem being used.
- Then ask pupils to find a group whose phrases might fit together. If there are any pupils left without partners/groups ask them to read their phrases to the class and see if the groups can identify where they should go and why.
- Ask pupils to identify who has the first and last lines of the poem. How do they know? What is the title of the poem? How do they know?
- Give out a copy of the full poem and read it aloud. Ask pupils in groups to talk about a number of questions relevant to the poem being studied. For the poem 'Shopping with the Buddha', for example, the questions might include:
  - What clues are there as to the poet's attitude to the Buddha?
  - What attitudes does the Buddha reveal through his behaviour?
  - What surprises are there in this presentation of the Buddha?
  - Compare the poem with an image of the Buddha. How far does the poem reflect the image?
  - Compare the poem with some texts from Buddhist scriptures. What connections can pupils make?
  - Choose three phrases that sum up the message of the poem.
  - How relevant are the teachings of a master from the sixth-century BCE to the life of a London poet? To what extent is it possible for the Buddha to fit into twenty-first century society? To both questions, give three positive responses, three critical views and one question of their own.

Useful for
Interpreting texts; developing understanding of the impact of beliefs on people today.

See also

Transporting character–8
Disentangling–107
Online resources PDF

110 Turn one thing into another

Strategy

- Provide pupils with a stimulus and ask them to re-present from a different perspective: for example, a documentary which they must turn into a campaign (for or against); a fictional dramatisation which they must turn into a news item; an eyewitness account which they must turn into a poem.
- Expect pupils to use the literary conventions of the text type they are transforming the writing into, but ensure that, even more importantly, they convey the religious or ethical material and any interpretation of the material.

Useful for
Processing material; developing deep understanding.

See also

Mysteries–49
Target board–94
Jigsaw reading–99

Useful for

Encouraging critical thinking about texts, stories and images.

See also

Fact or opinion–102
Disentangling–107
Perspectival reading–112

111 Form criticism

Strategy

- Provide pupils with a piece of text, a story or an image which is significant for the unit of work they are studying. Working in pairs or small groups, pupils work out what must have been happening at the time the text, story or image was produced (the *sitz im leben*, or 'setting in life'): for example, 'What must have been going on for these rules to have been given?' or 'How were people behaving if Jesus needed to tell this story?'
- Then pose a range of ideas and questions for pupils to respond to, linking the stimulus material with contemporary life.

Examples:

- Hindu guidelines for living (Hinduism). Follow-up question: Why are these rules needed? (What is the opposite of these ideas for being good?) Choose four or five ideas. Then describe a situation where it would make a difference if people followed these Hindu ideas.
- The Ten Commandments (Judaism). Follow-up question: What might the world be like if people genuinely followed God's commands?
- A summary of Guru Nanak's teaching (Sikhism). Follow up question: What would change in your school/community if people followed this teaching?

Useful for

Deepening understanding of texts; enabling recognition of how and why people interpret texts differently.

See also

Transporting a character–8
Target board–94

112 Perspectival reading

Strategy

- Choose a story relevant to the unit of work pupils are studying in which there are different perspectives among the main characters. See some examples below.
- In pairs, pupils read through the story from one of these perspectives:
  - You are [main character(s) – type 1]
  - You are [main character(s) – type 2]
  - You are a committed [member of the religion whose story it is] from today.
  - You are a wealthy, pleasure-seeking celebrity or sportsperson from today.
  - You are an agnostic, so you are unsure about [key issue in the chosen story].
  - You are an atheist, so you believe that there is no God. You do not value religious stories very much and are quite hostile to religion.
- Pupils respond in writing to the following questions from the perspective of the character above:
  - Why does this story interest you?
  - What do you think is the main reason?
  - What advice for living can you come up with from this story?

Examples:

- The Buddha's Last Sermon (Buddhism)
- Parable of the Unforgiving Servant (Christianity)
- The Churning the Ocean of Milk (Hinduism)
- Prophet Muhammad's (pbuh), Last Sermon (Islam)
- King David and Nathan the Prophet (Judaism)
- A King Learns How to Find God (Sikhism)

113 Silent conversations

Strategy

- Choose a poem which is relevant to the topic that pupils are studying and which offers the poet's insights and thoughts on life from the perspective of faith, e.g. 'Eleven Addresses to the Lord No1' by John Berryman (see: http://bit.ly/14PKIUD).
- Put verses of the chosen poem on large sheets of paper around the room.
- Pupils move around the room, writing in black ink their first responses to a phrase in the extracts or to the extracts as a whole. They can also comment on other people's comments.
- Give out some coloured pens to different pupils and ask them to add to the comments: blue pens (write questions); red pens (only allowed to challenge comments); green pens (qualify and extend comments).
- Each group of pupils then takes a 'conversation' (one of the large sheets of paper with annotated extracts from the poem). They consider how the extract communicates the poet's faith and the impact it has on the poet's life.
- As a class, pupils put the poem together and read it aloud.
- As individuals or pairs, pupils produce written responses to the following:
  - Choose two religious figures you have studied and one atheist person you know about. Summarise in 20–30 words each what they might say in response to the poem.
  - Write a letter to the poet. Express your own responses to the poem and the poet's beliefs – both critical and creative responses.

Useful for

Interpreting texts.

See also

Bag of words–109
Form criticism–111

114 Buttresses

Strategy

- Provide pupils with a series of five statements about an issue they are studying. They will also need a framework in which to record their responses with the headings: experience; reasons; sources of authority; arguments; my point of view. A template is provided in the online resources PDF.
- Ask pupils to choose one of the five statements and write it in the section 'My point of view'. They then try to justify their viewpoint by writing into the appropriate spaces in the template an experience, some reasons, an argument and a source of authority that supports their point of view.

Example: Some statements to get pupils thinking about Jewish identity

- 'Jewish identity is more about celebrating festivals and visiting holy places than about helping others or believing in God.'
- 'It is easy to be both British and Jewish.'
- 'If everyone copied Jewish family values, then Britain would be a better place.'
- 'My commitments and values are very similar to those of young British Jews.' (alternatively, 'completely different from').
- 'In Judaism, tradition matters more than change.'

Useful for

Supporting (buttressing) ideas with reasons, experience, sources of authority or arguments.

See also

Tenuous links–101
Fact or opinion–102
Online resources PDF

Buttresses: a metaphor for what students do with their viewpoints

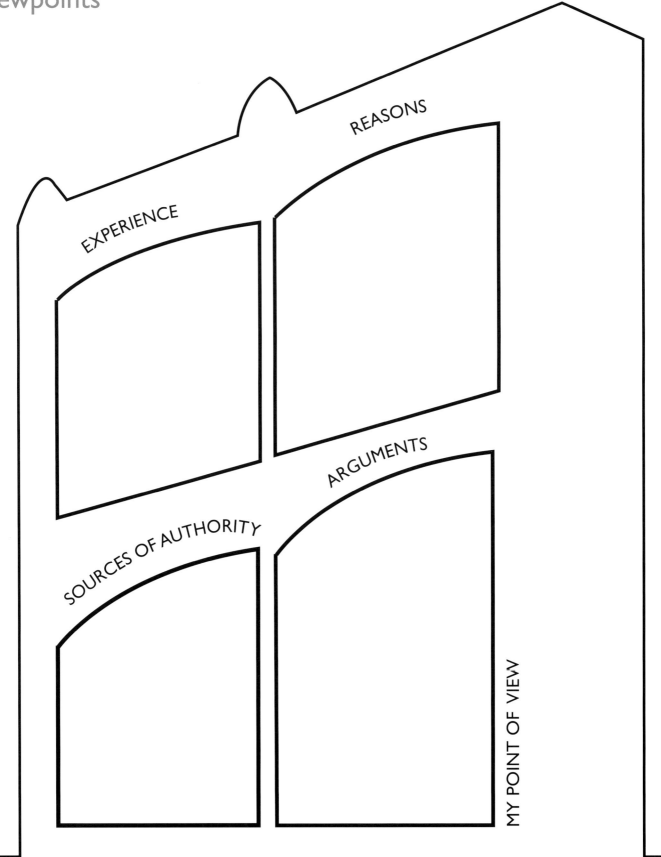

EXPERIENCE

REASONS

SOURCES OF AUTHORITY

ARGUMENTS

MY POINT OF VIEW

Photocopy permission

115 Socratic questioning

Strategy

- Organise the class into groups of 4–6. Give each group:
  - a key question to which they must work out a response
  - set of six question cards which provide a list of questions for each of the six types of questions which are part of the Socratic method (see no. 115 and the online resources PDF).
    - Questions of **clarification** and **refinement**
    - Questions that help **identify any assumptions** that have been made
    - Questions that are looking for **reasons** and **evidence**
    - Questions which **explore consequences and implications**
    - Questions that **seek out viewpoints and perspectives**
    - Questions **about the question**
  - a recording sheet (see the online resources PDF).
- Explain to pupils that this method of questioning is named after the classical Greek philosopher Socrates who used enquiry and debate to stimulate discussion with his fellow Athenians (his 'students'). In their groups, one pupil is to take on the role of 'student' and the others take on the role of Socrates as the 'questioners'. The questioners need to look for opportunities to ask the different types of questions, and the 'student' provides a response.
- The group records their discussion – either 'as they go' or at the end when an answer to the question has been identified.

Examples:

- Question: Why do some people believe/not believe in God?
- Stimulus materials: Give pupils a short account from Richard Dawkins and/or Alister McGrath arguing against and for belief in God.
- Activity: Pupils look through the account(s) in groups of three or four, using the Socratic questioning prompts, in order to answer the question.

Useful for

Using enquiry and debate to stimulate discussion and deep thinking; using rigorous questioning; looking for evidence in answers; challenging assumptions.

See also

Mysteries–49
Balloon debate–79
Online resources PDF

116 Different audiences

Strategy

- Film clips are often written with a specific audience in mind. Watching them from a variety of viewpoints can reveal new insights.
- Ask pupils to review film clips from different perspectives: for example, from people sympathetic to or those hostile to the message; from characters involved in the storyline or those who are neutral observers.

Useful for

Clarifying thinking; developing skill of empathy; encouraging consideration of views other than one's own; considering reasons for differences in beliefs.

See also

Create a cover–28
Human barchart–102
Tenuous links–101

Socratic method: question cards

Identify any assumptions

- What assumptions do you think the writer makes?
- What assumptions have we made?
- Can you explain why you think s/he assumes that?
- Why do you think she said that / used that phrase?
- Can we look at that in a different way?

Consequences and implications

- Does what you say fit with what we have already learnt about…?
- If s/he believes … then what difference would it make?
- If you are right about that then …?
- Would that make any difference?
- What are the implications of …?
- What would be the consequences of that?
- How could you test your theory?

Questions about the question

- Do you have any questions about the question?
- What is your general answer to the question?
- Do we need to record more than one view?
- Could we split this question up to make it clearer?
- How has our discussion so far helped us answer …?
- Who can summarise the points we have made so far?
- Can we now answer the question?

Clarification and refinement

- Why did the writer say …?
- What did the writer mean by …?
- Did he mean … or …?
- Can you give me an example of … ?
- What does the image/phrase … mean to you?
- Can you explain …?
- How did you think … would affect …?

Reasons and evidence

- What evidence do we have to support that view?
- How do we know …?
- Show me where in the text it says …
- What are your reasons?
- Why do you think … happened?
- How can you be sure that you are right?
- Is that enough evidence to say that …?
- Can you put it another way?

Viewpoints and perspectives

- Are you sure that …?
- Is there a different way of looking at that?
- What if …?
- If you are right about that, then why …?
- What would someone who disagreed with you say?
- What are the similarities and differences between our views/ideas?
- Are there any weaknesses in that theory/argument?

Index of strategies

Note: Numbers refer to Strategies not pages.

Faith stories

Faith stories are a fundamental part of RE, and so they feature as suitable stimuli in many of the strategies in *More Than 101 Great Ideas*. On this page is a list of all the stories mentioned, with a reference to other RE Today publications where you will find a version of the stories and suggestions for their use.

- **Faith Stories Collection** is a collection of 50 stories from the six principal religions, each reproduced on a side of A4 together with some suggested activities or questions to ask. Each story is available separately as a download (PDF) for £1. See: http://shop.retoday.org.uk
- **RE Today's series of curriculum publications** feature a variety of stimulus materials together with practical and engaging classroom strategies for using them. The series that feature the stories referred to in this publication are: Developing Primary RE (DPRE), Exploring a Theme (EAT), and Opening Up RE (OURE). See: http://shop.retoday.org.uk

Story	Strategy	Publication
Buddhism		
Angulimala and the Buddha	7	Faith Stories Collection; DPRE Faith Stories
Kisagotami and the Mustard Seed	7	Faith Stories Collection
Sunita the Scavenger	14	OURE Respect
Queen Maya's Dream	33, 73	Faith Stories Collection; DPRE Faith Stories
The Life of Siddhartha Gautama	97	Faith Stories Collection
Buddha's Last Sermon	112	Faith Stories Collection
Christianity		
The Nativity	7, 72	Faith Stories Collection; DPRE Christmas;
Pentecost	7	Faith Stories Collection
Jesus and Zacchaeus	14	EAT Beliefs in Action
Holy Week and Easter	24, 50, 97	Faith Stories Collection; OURE Easter;
The Feeding of the 5000	25	Faith Stories Collection
Parable of the Lost Son	33	Faith Stories Collection; OURE Christianity
Parable of the Unforgiving Servant	112	Faith Stories Collection
Genesis 1 Creation Story	73	Faith Stories Collection
The Walk to Emmaus	99	Faith Stories Collection
Hinduism		
Durga and the Buffalo Demon	7	Faith Stories Collection; DPRE Stories about God
The Story of Prahlad	7	Faith Stories Collection; DPRE Stories about God
Krishna Steals the Butter	24	Faith Stories Collection; DPRE Words of Wisdom
How Ganesha got his Elephant Head	73	Faith Stories Collection; EAT Sacred Stories
The Exile and Return of Rama and Sita	97	Faith Stories Collection; OURE Hinduism
The Churning of the Ocean of Milk	112	Faith Stories Collection
Islam		
Sheikh Abdul Qadir	63	Reflections: Strategies to Support Spiritual and Moral Development
The Night of Power	97, 99	Faith Stories Collection; OURE Islam
Muhammad's Last Sermon	112	Faith Stories Collection
Judaism		
Elijah and the Cave	7	Faith Stories Collection
The Ten Commandments	7	DPRE Stories; DPRE Stories about God
Abraham and Isaac	24	Faith Stories Collection; DPRE Faith Stories
Hanukkah	72	Faith Stories Collection; EAT Celebrations
Passover	97	DPRE Special Times; EAT Sacred Stories
King David and Nathan the Prophet	112	Faith Stories Collection
Sikhism		
Bhai Kanhaiya	7	Faith Stories Collection
Sajjan the Thief	7	Faith Stories Collection; EAT Codes for Living
Guru Nanak Lost in the River	33	Faith Stories Collection;
The Story of Baisakhi and Guru Gobind Singh	97	Faith Stories Collection; OURE Sikhism
The Birth of Guru Nanak	73	Faith Stories Collection
The Founding of the Khalsa	99	Faith Stories Collection; DPRE Faith Stories
A King Learns How to Find God	112	Faith Stories Collection